Our Psychic and Spiritual Journeys

BY

LOUISE MORGAN

Contents

Dedication

To my hubby, Mick, whose willingness to help and support me over the last 54 years on this amazing spiritual journey. I thank him for his constant and continuous support of putting this book together and for having to share his home, which became an "Open Door" for clients. Also, all the work he has contributed, i.e. Auragraphs, Healing Manuals and the endless computer work.

I thank you all from the bottom of my heart.
Love and Blessings

Louise Morgan xxx

Acknowledgements

I am indebted to the family and friends who have contributed to this book and without whose input this would not have been possible.

Their amazing stories were full of honesty, inner strength, courage and determination in unlocking their inner most thoughts and painful memories to bring this book together.

I hope this book will give others the courage and strength to bring enlightenment to their lives in their darkest moments.

To Marcella for our undying friendship through the struggles and laughter of reading, editing and re-editing in putting this book together.

Chapter 1

<u>Louise</u>

My first memory of something strange happening to me was in my family home, which I shared with my Mom, Dad, 3 brothers and 2 sisters. I was about 10 years old at the time, and I was fast asleep in bed and was awoken by 3 loud raps on the bedroom window. I remember screaming out as I thought somebody was trying to get in through the window. My Dad came in to see what was wrong, and I told him, but he said there was no one there and to go back to sleep. Thinking back, I remember my Mom, who was in hospital expecting another baby, but he was never brought home. Later, when I was older, Mom said it was a baby boy still born. I think now, as I have got older, it was when he had passed that I heard the knocking. Something similar happened when my Nan passed away, and now if I ever hear 3 raps, I know it is a warning someone will be taken over to the other side.

As I grew up, not much else happened. However, my first experience at Clairvoyance started at a party as a joke. We were discussing how my friend's new fella had fallen for her; someone said how do you know, and my sister said she reads palms (which at the time I didn't), so for a bit of fun, I picked up the girls palm and looked in and to my surprise saw a man with a beard standing outside a front door. I told her what I could see, and she said that's my fella. I then told her I thought she would get back with him, not knowing they had split up. The rest of the night was spent with me reading people's palms, telling them numerous things that were going to happen.

6 months later, at another party, I was told the thing I had said at the previous party had come true; however, I couldn't remember what I had said and wondered if I should be telling people these things. I went to visit a psychic fayre in the city I lived in. Whilst I was there, I saw a medium doing some readings and booked an appointment to see her for some advice. I mentioned what I had seen in other people's palms which they confirmed as true. She said while you are here, you can do me a palm reading. I could see visions of 2 people I described to her, and she confirmed they were her son and daughter. After the reading, she said that it is clairvoyance to see with the 3rd eye, it is a gift, and she told me to do everything, the cards, crystal ball, and the runes. I took her advice, and 40 years on, I am still doing this. Many more amazing spiritual journeys opened for me since that night many moons ago.

Little did I know how much more work I would be doing on my spiritual pathway, and I have had such an amazing journey, meeting lots of lovely people on my way. I started doing readings for family and friends whilst bringing up my 4 children and also working at many numerous jobs, being an Avon lady, working at the race courses taking bets. I started sitting in a circle with a lady I got to know who lived on the next road to me. She told me she had seen a ghost standing on the landing when she was in bed, and it turned out to be an aunt of hers who had passed away many years ago. As we chatted, we decided we would go to a spiritual church and see if there were any messages for us from the medium who was working that day. The medium came to my friend and said she should work on the platform herself, we were quite surprised, but years later, we were both on the platform giving proof to people of their families in the spirit world or, as I say, they are upstairs on the spiritual realms. We sat in a spiritual circle for many years at my friend's house. When I first sat for meditation in a spiritual circle, I was taken out of my body, and it was as if I was standing on the moon looking down on the earth. It was like a camera filming future events which were going to happen on the earth plane. The first thing I saw was a scene where I was in a horse-drawn carriage in Russia, being pulled through the snow. In front of me, I saw a huge explosion like an atomic bomb going off. I returned from the meditation quite shocked after what I had seen. Not long after this, there was an explosion in Russia, and it was Chernobyl. I couldn't believe it when I saw the news it was exactly what I had been shown. After this, I saw many events at our weekly meditation circle before they happened on the earth plane. One of these events I saw 18 months before it happened. I felt I was standing on a beach during my meditation and saw a boat that looked like a cruise ship. In monthly meditations, I was getting visions of future events yet to happen. I saw a huge hole in the front of a boat, and I thought something was going to happen to the QE2. I asked my husband if I should ring them, and he said yes if you want to, but I don't think they will take much notice. However, a week later, the boat I had seen was the Zeebrucker going down with the doors not closed and the water pouring in, I was so shocked and wished I had known more information before the event so I could have warned them, but it never happens like that as it seems it is meant to happen.

I started to experience more visions and pick up things that were about to happen. One evening I was sitting having my tea on a tray in the living room. I saw a vision of someone pushing a hospital trolley with my dinner on and thought I would be going into the hospital. Later that evening, as I had a shower, I found a lump in my breast and knew straight away I would be going into hospital. Fortunately, it was good news. The lump was benign, thank God. I then felt I was on the earth to do future spiritual/healing work.

3

When I first started my clairvoyant work, I saw lots of upsetting things, which I now understand you do take more notice of them as they register in your mind, and when they come to pass, you know you have seen them, but if it was a lottery win, you think it is more of a coincidence. One of the first visions I saw when I was doing readings for my friends was a large sporran on a Scotsman's kilt, I thought she might be going to Scotland, but she said no, however, 2 weeks later, she went to the Lords Mayor Procession and there was a Scottish pipe band with many sporrans, we laughed about this later. I carried on doing readings for anyone who wanted a reading and was often amazed at what I saw that can happen in people's lives and sometimes take many years to come to pass, sometimes 15/20 years. There is no time in the spirit world; I do believe our life is already mapped out for us.

I started on my healing journey many years ago when Spiritual Healing was the only way to heal with the laying of hands. The first session I attended was amazing as I saw beautiful colours flowing down through me into the person who I had my hands on. Afterward, I was told by my spirit guides it was the healing colours the person needed to help them on their road to recovery. From that session, I joined a lovely Spiritualist Church where everyone was very friendly and always shared their knowledge with the novices. I sat in a spiritual awareness circle with people of like mind and started to progress with my mediumship work seeing spirit souls who linked to the people in the congregation in the church service. One afternoon whilst working at the spiritual church, I saw a lady from spirit who looked like the old Queen Mary. She had a high collared dress, a wide-brimmed hat in cream and lovely pearls around her neck. A man came and stood next to her with a walking cane, looking very dapper, he said he had been with the King in India. As I was doing this spiritual service in the middle of a big city,

4

I thought, who is going to know who I have just described? No one could connect with them. Then I was shown the old Caxton printing presses, which I passed on, and this had a link to the lady who was running this church. She said her family had a printing business for a long time, and they had started with them many years before. I learned a very good lesson that day, to always say what you see, what is being shown to you from the spirit world.

During a healing session in the church, I met a lovely spiritual man, William, who had recently lost his wife. During the session, he spoke about becoming a healer himself as he was very drawn to the energy and the healing which had helped him come to terms with his wife's passing. After he trained to become a Spiritual and Reiki Healer, we started to work together doing healing every week at church. My friend Jean received a message from the spirit guides that she would be a medium which she was. Jean said we could use her healing room which we did every week. We also worked at my house but felt it was time to rent a room to carry on our healing and also teach people the healing energies of spiritual and reiki healing.

Another friend who was interested in Clairvoyance had seen an advert for a church which we could rent, and we liked the sound of so we joined up and met a lot of spiritual people. I found I was progressing well with this knowledge, so I suggested we teach courses on spiritual awareness, which covers many areas, i.e. learning the chakra system, the auric field, the energies and colours around the body, dowsing, crystals, tea leaf reading and palmistry. In the rooms we rented, many, many people have passed through the doors, with lots of them going on to teach awareness and taking courses on different therapies, Counselling, Reflexology, Indian Head massage and many more. Through my experience, I have found it is like throwing a stone into a pool and watching the ripples going out further and further to touch many people. Through my friend, Jean, I met a lady who, like myself, had many spiritual experiences, and we soon became very good friends. One day we were out in her car going to see a property she and her husband were looking to purchase, and whilst driving along, she drew a picture from someone in spirit she thought belonged to me. As I looked at it, I sensed the energy coming from the picture and said that I felt it was more to do with her hubby, who may know more about it. He confirmed by the description and the personality that it was his mother.

We decided to get together with some friends of mine and do some spiritual drawings to see what would come through. We were amazed to see all the drawings were so different, and all the energies from the spirit who came through gave proof it was genuine Many of the pictures were taken when they were younger and not as they looked when they passed away, but if we were to show photos of ourselves, it would be when we looked out best, wouldn't it?

On one occasion, we were working at a church doing a service when I said to my friend, Vera, I can see a man next to you from the spirit world with a very flashy coloured tie, and she said she could feel his presence and started to draw him. When I looked over at the picture, he said to me I was better looking than that; when I told Vera, she replied she couldn't do any better; however, when we showed it to the congregation at the spiritual church, he came through and spoke to me about his life as a healer. He worked with crystals, and he could see into the body when he was healing. He gave his name as Ivor James, and I knew that he was a healer, but I didn't know he had passed away. I passed this information on to the congregation at the church, and I said I didn't think he had passed away. One of the ladies came back and said he had passed away 6 months ago. What a privilege to have Ivor come and speak to us. I still have his picture that Vera drew, a lovely man and an amazing Spiritual healer. We carried on working with the spiritual drawings till Vera eventually bought a property down south and moved away.

I carried on working with my readings and got to know a lady named Dee, who I worked with in the bookmaker's shop, not far from where I lived, and I got a job with her where we had a lot of fun as well as marking the board and taking bets. We talked about reading palms and the cards, my friend's mom was very interested in the spiritual side of life, and she used to go to the Institute in Digbeth to see the spooks, as she called them. Dee decided she would like to come and join the circle with me at Jean's house and loved picking up the energies, and Jean advised us who our guides were.

One day when we were at work, Dee said there was strange energy she was picking up and I could see a bomb going off, and Dee saw a train crash. That evening on the news was the Brighton bomb, and a train crash had also happened that day. To say the very least, we were both shaken up at what we had seen happening that day. I still see Dee, and she still sits in a circle with me, she has brought her spiritual gift forward, and her story is a chapter further on in the book.

As I was finishing a clairvoyant reading at home, I felt Spirit was impressing me to get something together to open a shop which I couldn't see happening, but Spirit can always help if it is meant to be. My son, Jack, wanted to go into town and look for a coat to wear as he was going to start college. We found a shop which sold a lot of second-hand clothes which the students loved. Whilst I was there, I saw a lovely stall selling beautiful crystal earrings and necklaces, and I thought this would be ideal for the shop. I spoke to the lady about buying some of her jewellery and ordered some to pick up the following week. When I went to collect the order, she asked me if I would like to take on the stall and pay for it monthly, she said she would do me a good deal on the crystals. I was amazed and said yes straightaway; we named the stall The Zodiac Parlour, and my son, who is very good at art, did a poster to put in the window. My friend Jean and I did clairvoyant readings and had many clients coming to see us. Including the local stall holders and shopkeepers. I met a lady, Mia, at an astrology class, and she was a Tarot card reader. She also did readings with us. We were also trying to make customers aware of the healing and introducing crystals for healing. We got to know a very spiritual man who travelled from Worcester and advised us he was guided to us by his Spirit guides. He said he had got things to tell me. I was excited to hear what he had to say as I was always telling people things in their readings but never had a message myself. He was very well travelled and had been to India when the hippy trail had started with the Beatles going out there. On one of his visits, he had a traffic accident with the coach and couldn't walk. On his return home, he felt drawn to go to a Spiritualist Church in London, where he then lived. After several healing sessions he received at the church, he was able to start walking again, and he joined the Church and became a Spiritual Healer. He said that he too saw visions and had picked up someone in the Royal family who was going to die but wouldn't say who, but as we know now, it was the lovely Lady Diana. It was years after his prediction that it happened. I knew straight away what he had seen. Whilst we were doing the readings in the Shopping Mall. We started to see the stall holders moving out and having shops and stalls elsewhere. It came to pass quicker than we thought when we got to work one Monday a month later, as there was a lock and chain on the door, they had shut the market down without notifying the stall holders. So that was the end of that story. I still see a lady who came to me for readings, and we always reminisce about our time there and laugh about what went on there.

I have always felt very drawn to Astrology, and Mia used to go to night school classes which I also started to attend, and I was smitten. I loved all the aspects of the birth charts, planets and what they mean in our lives. I met a friend, June, there, who loved the same things as I did Healing, Mediumship, and Astrology, so we used to meet up every week at the night school, and we would then have a get-together at Jean's house, and they hit it off straight away with June introducing us to a Reiki Master named Bob. We all decided to do the Reiki healing course and loved the attunement we received from him. After I received the Reiki 1 and 2 attunements, I joined up with William again, and we started a weekly healing day at my house, which took off, and we had clients coming in every week for healing.

At this time, we had bought a cocker spaniel puppy from a friend of mine who bred dogs, she was a lovely dog, and everyone coming for appointments was always fussing with her. One of the other puppies in the litter had poor eyesight and was deaf, so we ended up with 2 pups running around the house. The week after we adopted Holly, both the pups got into the Healing room and did a whoopsie behind the chair, so that ended the healing at home. We started to look for a room for our weekly healing sessions, and a friend told us about a room in the village where she lived. We made inquiries and moved our weekly healing sessions. We got together with a group of like-minded people and started sitting in a circle every week which quickly began to grow, so we ended up renting 2 rooms for different spiritual classes. It is amazing how many people have come through the doors and been helped and, in return, wanted to become healers and help other people. As I said earlier, it is like throwing a stone into a pond and watching the ripples going further and further. This is what happens when you work spiritually, all linking together and helping each other.

Whilst we were running the spiritual centre doing spiritual awareness classes, including spiritual and reiki healing and mediumship, we were very busy. Someone suggested we try for a lottery grant to help us get rooms to work in. We decided to give it a try and applied for a grant and had several meetings with the Lottery grant organiser and showed them our business plan, including the cost of renting the rooms and purchasing everything we needed to start up to offer Indian head massage, reflexology, spiritual healing, etc. We were delighted to be awarded a grant.

We opened the centre and also opened a small shop selling crystals, angels, books, and many more items. We didn't charge the clients who were able to have the therapies as it helped them with their problems. It was busy and lovely energies were built up in these rooms. We branched out with the healing going into local councils and offices to help with stress-related problems, also helping asylum seekers to have therapies that helped them with the traumas they were experiencing or had experienced in the war-torn countries they had fled.

We remained open for a couple of years without having to charge for our therapies. However, we were running out of money to pay the rent, so sadly, we had to give it all up. But as we know, as one door closes, another one opens, and we went back into the rooms we rented and carried on with the spiritual awareness classes and the afternoon of mediumship until the lockdown came to close all the spiritual churches down.

My early life was quite normal as you have to grow up quickly if you are the eldest sibling, and my mom had lost 2 baby boys through Toxaemia, which meant she was in the hospital for weeks at a time throughout the pregnancies, meaning a lot of things were left to me like the washing nappies and plenty of them, cooking, shopping and doing a paper round which was normal in those days to have some money for sweets and the Saturday matinee which was the highlight of our week.

My Nan came to live with us as it was common then to have relatives stopping at our house even though there were only 3 bedrooms and we slept 4 to a bed, and our blankets were our dad's overcoat or whatever would keep us warm. The problem with so many sharing a bed did not just have little room in the bed, but if anyone had nits, we all ended up having them. I remember the embarrassment at school at being called out of class to go and see the nit nurse, but you soon learned to get over things like that.

We loved the summer holidays from school, there was a family who had 11 children, and we used to go on picnics with them taking my 2 younger brothers, aged 1 and 2 years old, in the pram. We had jam sandwiches and water and walked over fields paddling in the streams looking for fish or frogspawn and swinging across the rivers on rope swings, all great fun, and then got home late for our dinner. My mom was sometimes depressed, so it was often a difficult situation as there was never enough money for what was needed. New clothes that were needed were always from a jumble sale, but everyone was in the same boat, and we all had gabardine macs.

The most exciting thing I remember was when we had a television with a small screen, and we all used to fight to get on the chair nearest to it. Watch with Mother, this programme brought peace to the house for a short time watching, also, Andy Pandy, Bill and Ben, The Wooden Tops, we loved them all.

I started work for British Rail in the offices doing clerical work, and my pay was £2.50, which Mom had £2, and I had the 50p (which was 10 shillings then), which paid for my Provident cheque and some for a night out at the youth club. Rock and Roll had just started to take off on the radio, Elvis, Tommy Steele, and Cliff Richard; we used to go jiving to this music and still do. The first time I heard the Beatles sing Love me do, I was smitten, and it was a new era of change from Rockers to Mods. Clothes and hairstyles and music changed, and it was a great time to be young with so much freedom to go clubbing and on holiday to Margate with all the Mods; I loved it.

I met my hubby, who was also a mod, and we just clicked and got married in 1967 and are still together 51 years later with 4 lovely children and 6 amazing grandchildren who we love to bits, also our lovely dogs, which have been great companions on this amazing journey. We realise now we are soul mates.

As my family has grown up and moved on with their lives, I decided to use the spare bedroom as a healing room and put all my crystals, Buddha, and books I collected over the years of working for Spirit. When we first began to sit in a circle, I would watch the people sitting, and I could see their guides and helpers from the Spirit World move behind them, connecting to their energy field. There were Nuns, Native American Indians, and Chinese Monks connected to the different people in the group. Moving into the early 1990s, there was a change in the energy called A Harmonic Convergence, and the energies changed, making it easier to connect with the different vibrations, and I was able to pick up the energy of the Egyptian vibrations. This was strong energy different to what had gone before. I always placed a large quartz crystal in the middle of the circle, which was good for group harmony. One night I was looking around the group. I saw an Egyptian Hand Maiden place a baby on the crystal; I knew it meant a grandchild for me. Not long after this, my eldest daughter told me she was expecting her first baby, which was a girl, and we were elated and absolutely over the moon. I said to my husband in the space of 6 that someone else was going to tell us they were expecting, and it was my son's wife 6 weeks later. Both babies were at my other daughter's wedding, all that excitement in 6 weeks. My other grandchildren were born 4 weeks and 6 months apart. A bit like buses, you never get 1, always 2 together. I think they are all done having babies now.

Around this time, the energies started to change, and the Angel vibration started to come in around a lot of people who were feeling the presence of Angels. At one time, you only saw angel statues in graveyards or churches, but they came through on a powerful vibration.

My first encounter with Angels was a sad time for me. I was washing up in my kitchen, and the thought came into my head that my Dad was going to die on my birthday as he hadn't been very well but seemed ok in himself. I asked Spirit, please don't take my Dad, not on my birthday. Over the next 2 weeks, Dad didn't seem to be the same and was walking very slowly. He was taken to hospital, but the doctors were unable to find anything wrong with him. One night after work, when everyone had gone to bed, I said a rosary for him, and into the living room came the spirit of his Mom and Dad. I thought they had come to help him get better, and when I saw Dad at the hospital the next day, he was sitting in the chair, and he seemed a lot better. Before I left him, I said I would be up tomorrow, which was my birthday, to do a jig for him, and as my Dad was Irish knew he would appreciate the music. However, true to Spirit's word, my Dad passed at 4 am the next morning. I was born on 17th March, St. Patricks Day, and my Dad went home on the same day; they must have had a Hooley that day, very apt for an Irishman to go home to his other family. I was devastated, even though Spirit had forewarned me; you never think you are going to lose your Dad. I couldn't even think about opening any cards or presents after that, but a strange thing happened.

A present someone gave me had rolled off the kitchen unit, and my husband didn't tell me it was a statue and part of it had broken off. He repaired it, and the next day I was crying on and off and went upstairs to get something, and on a table, there was a beautiful statue of an Angel, which was the present that had rolled off the unit. I was overwhelmed when I saw it, and the energy I felt from it was amazing. From this experience and the feeling of love from the Angel, I wanted to know more about the angelic realms and started to learn about the Angels and how they can help in our lives, and how to call on them if we are worried, upset or need healing feeling their amazing energy and love vibration. Also, how to use the Angel cards. I thought this would be a lovely journey to bring forward for people, so I thought I would start doing workshops and meditation classes for people to experience what I felt. There is an abundance of information and Angel cards on the Internet and many lovely books to read. Approximately 20 years ago, there wasn't that much information, but since then, we have been empowered by the Angels, and how lucky the generations are now to know they can learn and connect to the Angels.

As I mentioned earlier, we had 2 lovely Cocker Spaniel dogs that were like our babies. One of them suffered quite a bit with her tummy, and she used to have a light chicken diet. One night we woke up, and she was walking around the bedroom panting. We were so worried we took her to the vet, who gave her some tablets which helped but didn't cure her. One evening she was not well and lying on her bed, so I sat beside her to give some healing, and around her bed stood a group of the Little Folk, the Fairies, and Gnomes. I carried on giving healing, and she went into a deep sleep; I'm sure she sensed their energy just as I did, and I gave thanks to them for coming to help me. We took her back to the vets a couple of weeks later, and they said she needed an operation which we booked her in for. The night after the operation, I was so worried about her and wondered if she would come home to us.

My hubby came into the bedroom and said he picked up the energy of a leprechaun who said, "Ahh, she'll be ok" in an Irish voice; we were over the moon with the message. 2 days later, she came home much better and able to eat any food she liked.

After that experience of seeing the Little Folk, I looked for a book to read as I wanted to know more about their energy and the vibration they work on. I found a book called Summer with the Leprechauns, and I started reading it in bed, and then my hubby got into bed. He asked me what I was reading, and before I could answer, he said, I can see a creature like a Leprechaun with pointed ears and a hooked nose; it came up to the bed and took his hands and rubbed soil in them. My hubby said he was ugly; I said don't say that he'll hear you. I must say if you are interested in knowing more about the Fairy realms, it is worth a read.

Another experience I had was when I was asked to give healing to a horse that had a very sore eye. When I arrived at a lovely big country house, the lady I had previously chatted to over the phone came to the door and took me to the stables at the back of the house, where I was introduced to a beautiful white horse. I started to do some Reiki healing on her with a crystal. I picked up she wanted a foal, and her injured eye had stopped her from doing what she was trained for. I explained to her owner what I had picked up, and she said to me she would have a lovely foal but was not sure if she could put her through the ordeal. Her eye stopped watering after the healing. I felt that the horse in the next stable wanted me to go to him, I placed my hands on him, and I picked up his energy and felt he was letting me know something about not hearing music anymore. I told the owner what I had picked up from him, and she said the other horse hadn't been trained for dressage for the last 6 months because of her eye problems, so the music hadn't been played around the stable. What a surprise, another example of always saying what you pick up, such powerful energy from horses. They can tell you about their illnesses and what has happened to them.

Another example of animal healing is a lady who came to me for occasional readings and said her dog had not been well and had a sore mouth. When I put my hands on him, I felt he was telling me he had not had his Quaker Oats; when I told his owner what I had picked, she laughed and said this was correct as he hadn't had any for about 6 months. I told her he wanted to start eating them again.

The dog sat very quietly when he had the healing, and I told her the prescription for him was a piece of amethyst crystal in his drinking water. His sore mouth improved, and I'm sure he had his Quaker Oats back.

My eldest daughter, Lucy brought a lovely little Cocker Spaniel into our home one day; she had a lovely gentle nature. My daughter had moved to a different part of the country with her boyfriend, and their relationship was a bit rocky, but she decided to give it another go. She rang me one Saturday afternoon to say the dog had a nosebleed and was taken to the vet and asked if I could send some healing straight away. I picked up my healing crystal and started to send healing, but the healing energy wouldn't start; Spirit said what will be will be. I was shocked as I hadn't had this happen to me before, so I asked them what they meant and was told it was to bring her back home. I didn't tell her what I had experienced, and the next time she rang it was to say her lovely dog had died of a brain haemorrhage, it was such a shock and the following day she came back over to our house, we were so upset, and my daughter stopped over that night and slept on a bed in the healing room. I went in to see her before I went to bed and I saw huge energy of white light come and stand behind my daughter, it was an earth goddess who explained to us that the dog was ok now over with all the other dogs and that our dogs don't always understand what we say to them, but when they are all together they are fine. What a privilege to have been given this knowledge; although it didn't make the loss any easier, the Goddess did leave us with a feeling of peace.

I then saw in my daughter's tea leaves that she was coming home, and I could see a small house with a lightbulb hanging on a long flex. She then went to view a house to rent not far from ours,

17

and when she got there, the light was on, and the bulb was hanging on a long piece of cord. We laughed and said there's no need to view the property as you will have it, and she moved back for a reason, but it was a very painful experience. My daughter picks up a lot of spiritual energy now herself and can also read the tea leaves and palms, like Mother, like Daughter Bless.

Lucy, my daughter, had a big birthday in 2017, and we were talking about where to go and what to do to celebrate it when I looked at Lucy and saw her Nan next to her, and she showed me an image of the Statue of Liberty on the kitchen wall. I told Lucy it looks like you are going to America. She said, "I don't think so, Mom". However, a few weeks later, a deal came up on Black Friday, and it was a cheap holiday to New York, and Lucy was able to book it, so her Nan was right when she stood beside her and showed me the vision – many thanks to Spirit.

Many years ago, when my family was growing up, my Hubby did a competition in a local Trade magazine he used to receive once a month. We sat one evening in the winter trying to decide the words needed in verse to win £2,000 or a holiday to Hawaii. 3 months later, on my Hubbie's 40th birthday, we had a phone call to say he had won the competition. I thought the caller was joking until she repeated back to me the verse that had been sent in; we were over the moon and decided to have the £2,000, which we immediately booked our first holiday in Spain. We were smitten and loved the ambiance and the Manyana way of life, so we started looking for places to buy over there, pipe dreams like everyone has. I used to send my thoughts out occasionally about having a bolt-hole abroad.

One day I saw an advert in a newspaper for caravans for sale in Spain, so we booked a holiday and went to have a look, they were very small places, so we left and came home. I went to get something out of my kitchen cupboard, and a photo of a caravan fell out onto the kitchen floor. I picked it up and heard the month of October mentioned. I thought I might go on holiday then but never looked at any holidays as my Mom had had a bad stroke in August. We were all devastated as she could only say a couple of words, and she was never the same after that. As I was on my way to see her in the hospital one day, a voice told me to get the local newspaper, and I thought, what do I want with that again? The voice said get a certain newspaper and believe it or not, but at the time, I was passing a paper shop. I went in and bought the newspaper, and later that week, I opened it at a page showing caravans for sale abroad. I looked down the list and saw some for sale in Portugal, and we had been there the year before and loved it. I rang the next day and spoke to the Company who was selling the caravans. He said he was starting to put caravans on a site that was already established. We asked if we could bring our dogs over, and he said yes, so we decided to go and see what was for sale and were pleasantly surprised. The caravan site was beautiful, with palm trees and lovely gardens surrounding the caravans. A lot of people were already living there, and we loved it, and we arranged to buy a caravan from him straight away at a very reasonable price. We travelled with our dogs many times on the new scheme Pet Passport. It all fell totally into place with the help of the Spirit Guides telling me to get Daltons Weekly.

When I am in Portugal, the energy is very peaceful. I have written my Reiki manuals 1, 2, and 3; there are also many workshops, and now this book. I feel very privileged to be able to write this down with the help of my team of guides, helpers, and inspirers.

One evening we were having a meal at home, and my daughter, Danielle, was chatting about having a career break from work as she had worked in the same job for several years and fancied a change. We spoke about her going to Portugal with her dog and stopping in the caravan, so we started to make plans for the journey, and before we knew it, it all started to fall into place, and she was given the ok from work to take a career break. What she had thought was a pipe dream was now all falling into place as it was meant to be. We checked the ferry crossings and loaded the car up, and set off on a 3-day journey on the ferry and overland. The start of a lovely adventure, and then we arrived at the caravan, and the first couple of weeks were spent settling into this lovely way of life.

Danielle was talking about getting a part-time job when Hubby and I went home 6 weeks later. She had taken a few telephone numbers from home for holiday companies she had been looking at and thinking about which to ring first. Into her head came ring Cosmos. It was so clear and such a surprise as Danielle had never had anything like that happen to her before. She rang the company, and they asked her to go for an interview that week; she started work 2 days later and met a lot of lovely people, making her time spent in Portugal something to always remember. After she came home from Portugal, we were chatting one night about yoga classes; she said she would like to start this and keep her fitness up. She joined a gym where yoga classes were included in the monthly subscription. She enjoyed the classes, and after a couple of years, she thought about becoming a yoga teacher. She started a course to become a Yoga teacher, which she passed with flying colours.

She now successfully runs several weekly yoga classes. She loves doing her classes, and during the Covid Pandemic, she decided to do some classes on Zoom, which was greatly received by her students. This has made her much more spiritually aware and given her greater insight into the spiritual side of life, which she shares with her students.

The house my Mom moved to after I left home and got married was always thought to have spirit people still living there. My youngest brother was about 10 years old and always used to say there was a black and white dog coming into the bedroom. We used to make fun of him and say the next thing he says he sees will be pink elephants. In the back bedroom, my other brother would say there was a strong smell of onions, and he used to feel someone holding his hand. I told him the next time this happens, send your thoughts out and say who are you, he did just that, and a name came back – Mary Matthews, and this unnerved him.

I used to look into the garden and felt it had been a farm with the dog being a sheepdog. One afternoon in the summer, we went to a garden fete where there was a lady who had looked into the history of the surrounding areas where we had grown up. I asked her if she had any idea if there had been farms in the area and mentioned the road where Mom had lived. She said there was a farm there and it was called Quagmire Farm and she showed me photos of the farm, it was right in the area where my Mom's house was, how amazing. I mentioned I was clairvoyant and had seen things and asked her about the dog and what my family had experienced when they lived there. She said there had been reports of people seeing a man with a sheep dog walk through the recreation ground, which was on the back of the houses, and when they looked again, he was gone. I thanked her for all her information and told my brothers about the farm and the black and white dog. We didn't realise it at the time, but it was my brother's spiritual energy opening as they both occasionally see people in the Spirit world now.

The first house I moved into when my 2 daughters were small was on a large housing estate called an overspill; it was quite a way from where I had been brought up, and I wasn't sure if I wanted to move that far from my family. We were given the keys to 3 different properties from the Housing office to go and view them. At the last house we viewed, I heard a voice as I went into the hallway saying you are going to live here I was surprised to hear that and thought I'm not sure if I want to live here. As I walked into the kitchen area, it had got the first fitted kitchen I had seen, and I thought I liked this. We went back to the office and handed the 2 sets of keys back, and said we would take our house.

One evening I had a fortune teller come to our house to do my family some readings, and she kept saying to me don't ever sell this house as it is special. I now know she was so right. After I had my last daughter, I was sitting watching the television when the family had all gone to bed. I had the image of a hospital trolley being pushed toward me. I thought I'm going to the hospital, but I felt ok. That evening I went for a shower and found a lump in my right breast. I thought I was mistaken, so I felt again, and it was definitely a lump. I went to the doctor, and he sent me to the local hospital, where I was told the lump should be removed; there were no scanners then, they used to take out the lump and test it, and if it was cancer, they took off your breast. I had to sign the consent form and was so frightened before the operation. I came around and looked down at the bedclothes to see a lot of black stitches, but thankfully it was from the lump being taken out. I was able to go home. When I saw my children, I was so relieved to think I had got my life to be able to bring them up and had come through this. I felt I had to do something with my life. I used to get awful smells occasionally, always knowing something bad would happen or someone was going to pass away. I had no idea what it was; I just had to wait and see.

I passed my driving test and loved the idea of getting in the car to go shopping and over to see my Mom. I hadn't been driving long and had a dog run into the side of the car, banging the back door, and then he ran off. I stopped the car and went to look for him, but he had run off. I was so shocked. 2 weeks later I was going to meet my sister for an evening out, but I had a funny feeling all day that things didn't feel right. I saw a pen on the unit in the kitchen and felt I needed to put it in my bag, but I thought what for and when I closed the front door at 7.30 to meet my sister the voice said you'll be glad when you are coming back. I started the journey feeling quite unnerved, and as I came to a busy junction on the road, ready to turn right, a driver drove into my car and turned the car right around. The battery shot out of the car and landed on the road, it must have been seconds, but it felt forever. A priest came over and asked me if I was ok; he had the long black habit on. I wondered if he was a protecting guide as when I looked down at myself as I got out of the car, I had a small cut on my left leg.

The Policeman asked me if I knew how lucky I was to come out of that accident with just that small cut; I thought after that happened, I won't drive again. When I went home and saw my children in bed all safe, I thought if anything had happened that night, I wouldn't have been there to care for and love them and bring them up.

One evening not long after that had happened, my sister popped in for a chat and cuppa; when it was time for her to leave, she said shall I take Vicky with me which was my youngest daughter, to our mom's house as I was going the next evening to see Mom and Dad. I said yes, ok, I can pick her up tomorrow night. As soon as her car disappeared out of sight, I had an overwhelming feeling that I must fetch her back. I thought how silly she was with my family; she would be ok. I couldn't clear the premonition. I didn't say anything but couldn't sleep properly that night with the thought of what I felt. As my hubby was getting ready for work, I told him I must go and fetch Vicky back but didn't know why; he said ok and dropped me over to my Moms house, and she was surprised to see me at the front door and asked me what's happened. I said I don't know, but I have come to take Vicky home; she said ok if that's how you feel. After we got into the car, the premonition lifted, and I started to think it was me being silly, but when I returned to see Mom and Dad that evening, Mom said in the afternoon, my brother had come down with his daughter who was about 4 years of age. They decided to go fishing in the canal near where my Mom lived. When my brother was leaning over to look at the fish, Dolly came behind him and pushed him into the canal. I knew then what the entire premonition was about. It would have been Vicky who would have been pushed in. I thanked my guides and helpers for what I had received from them and started to cry as I felt so overwhelmed.

I mentioned earlier in my book about Mom having a bad stroke; she recovered to a degree, but she was never the same again; she never regained her full speech, and we joined together as a family and looked after her every need, and she still loved a party and music. My Mom could sing a song but couldn't say a sentence, and doctors told us it was a different part of the brain used for singing.

I was washing up one morning and heard the words of the song "I'll be seeing you", and I thought that Dad was singing to me as he used to get up on stage in the pubs and sing. He had a good voice. I thought it was strange but had to go out, so I just got ready and forgot about it until I heard the words again later that week. It went like this. I'll be seeing you in all the old familiar places.

I heard it a few times that week and mentioned it to my hubby and said do you think I'm going to die or pop my clogs, he said he had heard the same song as well. 2 days later, my Mom fell and broke her hip she was taken into hospital and had a hip replacement but didn't recover that well and pneumonia set in and she passed away. We were heartbroken; my brother rang to tell me the news. I couldn't stop crying, and as I sat down, I heard a voice from the spirit say your mother is ok. I heard it 3 times and said is that you Dad? Then all the lights went out, and the TV went off. I knew then my Dad was trying to tell me in that song he sang to me. We had it played at Mom's funeral, knowing then she was with my Dad. I have seen my Mom in dreams, and she always looks much younger, and so does Dad. Bless them both.

From finding out about my clairvoyant gifts, my sisters also could read palms and also my daughter. My 2 brothers have seen people who are in spirit and said it is like they are looking at someone who is still living. My one brother was helping my hubby with a job taking out an old fireplace in a customer's house. At lunch time they stopped and sat down with the lady whose house it was. My brother said where's the old dear who was sitting in the armchair in the living room. She said my Mom used to live with us, but she passed away 2 years ago. The hair stood up on the back of his neck; he had seen her like she was when she was alive. My other brother lives in a house, and they are always hearing bells tingling, also he has seen a woman in the bathroom mirror that has a 1940's hairstyle and looks like she belongs to that era. He sometimes hears someone going down the stairs in the morning as if she is going to work, but they are used to all the noises, etc., and don't take any notice, all living happily together.

I was sitting in my healing room one afternoon after I had finished some healing and given thanks. Overpowering energy came into the room, and I felt they wanted to communicate some writings to me. I felt impelled to draw a triangle on top of the page and started to write words that I couldn't make out until I read it back to myself. The energy signed off with The Brotherhood of White Light which I knew nothing about. The guidance wrote many pages over a period of 18 months, and it turned out to be a book called Love is The Key which is a workshop book explaining how working with the geometric language of light, you can raise your vibration, open the energy field around your aura to work on the fifth vibration opening your heart to unconditional love. I was amazed to see what they had written through me, and the energy was always filled with love. I would love to bottle that energy and give it out so people can feel that vibration and the love.

Reiki

My first experience of healing happened by accident. My daughter's boyfriend had not been very well and had recently had a minor operation. He came to our house one Sunday afternoon, and I felt very drawn to put my hands on him to give healing. As I did this, I felt the top of my head open up, and energies of the colour blue poured into my head and down my arms into his shoulders. I just stood there until the energy stopped, and it was such a surprise. I felt very drawn to give healing after this experience, so I looked around for a healing course and found one in a church near where I lived. I thought Spiritual healing was the way forward and started a course. The healing energy is amazing and always different for each individual, with colours and energy coming into the client, and they often drift off into a sleep state, seeing different colours themselves. There are other energies around the bed, which are the healing guides and the peace and oneness which come with the healing are amazing.

After doing the course, I decided to start a Reiki healing course which started to come through in the area we lived in during the 90s. It is a different energy to spiritual healing, and you can take different levels of Reiki attunment, Reiki 1, 2, and the Masters; it is a lovely energy to work with and brings in more balancing energy for the clients helping to bring the chakras back into balance, making us feel at one with our spiritual body. Today we are on a treadmill, never having enough time for anything or anyone, or enough money. Nearly all our illness's come from emotional and mental issues we have experienced in our lives. Our bodies have 7 auras of light around it, linking to the spiritual body. The mental and emotional bodies soak up all the hurt and thinking about things we cannot change, so it goes over and over in our heads and seeps down into our physical bodies, which makes us ill. If this occurs in your life, write out all your upsets and disappointments and burn them, asking the angels to take all the negativity away, and you will eventually feel things lifting from you, and you can go forward in your life and make a fresh start. I have given this advice many times to people who have come to me for a reading, and they have told me how it worked for them to release negative energy.

Through spiritual healing, at Church, I met some lovely people, and we used to partner up together to give healing to clients. One lady was very spiritual, and we got on well; we used to work with a lady called Vera, who did spirit drawings and worked in a lot of the churches around our area.

I started thinking about running our church in rooms we rented to do spiritual awareness classes. Vera booked the mediums and the chairing for the mediums on the platform. We have been doing our services for over 20 years now with some lovely mediums, which we have welcomed into the church and have become great friends; it has been amazing proof from the afterlife. Our lovely families have been brought through people taking so much comfort knowing their families upstairs are never far away. It is amazing how much proof comes through when I am doing readings at my home, and spirit comes in as you never know what information they are going to give about the person and their families as they draw close to their loved ones during the reading.

I had a lovely lady, Amy, come to see me for a reading; her Nan had passed over some weeks before. She showed me she was with her sister, who had a long skirt on from the 1920s era. Nan proceeded to tell me about her first love when she was in her teenage years, saying how much she had loved him. Amy said as far as she knew, Nan was only with Grandad. The following day she rang her Mom who knew about her first love and sent her a photo of him on her mobile phone. He had passed away in a motorbike accident when he was young. She showed me the photo, and it was lovely to get proof of what Nan had spoken about. It must have broken her heart as she was nearly 90 when she died and spoke to me of her love for him. More information was given about how much she loved the granddaughter but could never say the words, and she was her favourite.

As I have said, all of my family have had some kind of spiritual experience. When my niece, Lois, started seeing an elderly man walking up the stairs in her house, she couldn't understand where he came from. She rang me, and I thought it was the former owner of the house. She saw him again in the bedroom one evening, and she jumped out of bed, turned the light on, and he disappeared. After this, she always had to have a lamp on in the bedroom. As time went on, she met a lovely guy, and they moved into a different area where the properties were older. She started to see a lot of different things in the flat, some not very nice.

You can read Lois' story later in the book.

In the early seventies, Ouija boards became very popular. My sister and I used it one afternoon for a bit of fun. I asked my Dad to give us a question we could ask the board but didn't know the answer to. We had an aunt who lived in Ireland and used to see her when we visited Dublin. Dad asked us to ask the board what her maiden name was, and it spelled out Brady, which was correct. Dad accused us of knowing it, but we didn't. A friend of ours, Malcolm, shouted from the kitchen to ask the name of the person I was going to marry, and it spelled out Gina, and he just laughed it off. However, on a fishing trip in Yorkshire, he met, who do you think? Yes, Gina and they hit it off immediately and are still together.

I decided to take the Ouija board back to my house, and we sat with it the following day. A friend of mine popped in for a cuppa, and I showed her the board, and she asked if she could take it with her and try it, which she did. The next day she brought it back, and she had a nerve rash on her neck and started to explain what happened the previous night. They put some candles on and turned off the lights asking the board, "Is there anybody there" and the glass started to move around the board, spelling out Claudius, a Roman soldier who had been murdered by Romulus and Helix. They put the board away as it frightened them. I took the board off her and left it on the porch, and never used it again. Some years later, a pub was built around the corner from where we lived, and we were 'gobsmacked' to see the name, which was The Centurion. STRANGER THAN FICTION!

I had a lady come for healing one afternoon; she came with her husband, Bill, who asked if he could sit in on the healing I was giving to his wife. As I started giving healing to his wife, I saw a man standing behind him who looked like Bill; when I finished the Reiki healing, I asked him if he believed in the Spirit world, and he said he was open to understanding more of what he had seen with the healing. I then told him I had seen a man standing behind him, whom I said was his Dad, and proceeded to tell him what he was saying, and Bill had never experienced anything like this before. He wanted to know more about how healing, clairvoyance, and mediumship worked. As he worked in the Police force, he only dealt with facts and reality and was interested in any workshops on the above-mentioned that I was teaching. A few months later, he came and sat in an awareness circle, which inspired him to learn and understand more of the spiritual dimensions.

From time to time, Bill brought me photos of people who had gone missing or were deceased. The visions I received of these incidents were very graphic and upsetting. Some of the information I received was extremely accurate and helped him marry up with the information he already had to get a fuller picture of what had happened and help guide him to the perpetrator.

I have often wondered where my gifts came from as my Dad didn't believe in anything spiritual and said when your dead, your dead, and you can bury me in the back garden. My Mom used to take the clairvoyant readings and healing but never picked up anything.

One day I was chatting to my Aunt in Dublin, and she started to tell me about her experiences of the spirit world, saying my other aunt, who had passed away, came to visit her one night and also her husband and brother. She made me laugh as she used to tell them to go away as she wanted to go to sleep. She said when she was a small child, she awoke one night to see a Viking standing by the fire; she had never forgotten it. Not long after that, there was a Viking boat found on the River Liffey. It was brought out and is now in the Dublin Museum. So the Vikings are still around us. She passed recently. She was 92. I have missed chatting to her about her life and her walks down memory lane; bless her.

When we lost our 2 lovely cocker spaniels, Meg and Holly, we were so upset as they were like our babies. Also, my daughter, Danielle, lost her cocker spaniel, Daisy, a few months after. We missed the dogs and their companionship terribly and decided we would not have another dog because of the heartbreak when you lose them.

I was reading Danielle's tea leaves one day, and I saw a lovely cocker spaniel pup at the bottom of her cup. I told her what I had seen, but she said she wasn't having another dog but had sent her thoughts out on the abundance list for a male companion. So we didn't discuss it any further. A few months later, she said if she had another dog, she would call him Darcy after Mr. Darcy from the series Pride and Prejudice. We decided to have a shopping trip out to another town about an hour's ride from where we lived. We were looking for a restaurant after we had finished our shopping, and Danielle said look at that lovely spaniel, Mom. We went over to give the dog some fuss. He was a lovely golden spaniel, and as we fussed him, he lay on Danielle's feet. We asked his name, which was Darcy, and we just looked at each other in shock. The lady had just bought him from a breeder in the next village and said there were 2 bitches there that had a litter each. We asked for the details and rang the breeder when we got home and made an appointment to see the pups the following day. There were 10 black pups and 2 golden, and they were all lovely, and we loved seeing them all together jumping and playing with each other.

The golden pup came straight over to Danielle, and she picked him up. He was the image of the dog we had seen in the town previously. She was smitten, and we said we would have the pups; I had a lovely little black bitch with a lovely little face. We enquired about the deposit, which was £300 each. Danielle paid £100, which she had with her, and advised we would sort out the balance the next day. That evening I was meeting friends at the local bingo. I wasn't doing any good crossing the numbers off when I heard a voice in my head saying I would win some money to buy the dogs. I started to cross off the numbers, and I shouted bingo, and another lady shouted with me at the same time. It was for £1000, so we had £500 each, just the amount we needed to get the deposit for the dogs. We paid the money the following day and went over 8 weeks later to pick up our lovely fur babies. I said to Danielle next time you send your thoughts for a male companion, mention he needs to have 2 legs, not 4, but she is very happy with her 4-legged lovely dog.

One day I had a vision as I was sitting in the healing room of 2 babies lying in 2 small Moses baskets. One was a baby about a month old, and the other was a new born. I said to my hubby I think we are going to have 2 new grandchildren, but I couldn't see if they were boys or girls. A couple of months later, my son's wife, Alice, rang to say they were coming over to see us on holiday. I was so excited to see my grandson, Oliver. When they arrived, he had grown so much. Alice gave me an envelope which I opened, and it was a scan of a baby. I was elated and said someone was going to tell me in the next few days they were pregnant. It was my youngest daughter, Vicky, who was expecting her first baby. How lovely 2 new babies coming into the family. Alice had a baby boy, and a month later, Vicky went into labour and went to the hospital, but they sent her back home as she had just started labour. She rang me to say she was back home and she had to go back when the pain got worse. I said ok, and I'll see you about 5.0.clock, and she said why do you have to say that and I replied it just came into my head. I walked into the labour ward at 5 am. She was just being born. Seeing my daughter in labour was awful. I said I wish I could have had her for you and would have had your pain. We all have to suffer in labour but look what we have at the end, our beautiful family who mean the world to us.

When my family had grown up and moved out of the family home. I decided to use their bedroom as a healing room which I regularly use for clients who come to see me for healing and meditation circles. One day after the healing had finished, I felt there was strong energy left in the room and felt I had to channel the words I was being given and started to write the words down. It was the first time I had ever done anything like this. I was writing down the words but did not understand what I was writing until I read it back to myself. I felt this was spiritual guidance explaining how the energy around the earth plane works, being all synchronized together to keep the planet we live on in balance. I was truly amazed at what I had written, and this happened continually over 18 months; it turned out to be a workshop book for raising our vibrations to a higher level and making us think more about the world we live in, including the animal kingdom and the land which we are destroying. They advised me the title of the book is to be **LOVE IS THE KEY** which is very true. It is a workshop book to open our hearts to the human race, which is needed now more than ever.

Chapter 2

Gary

As far back as I can remember, I recall being taken into someone's home, given something to eat, and then led up some stairs by soft, gentle female hands and taken to a room with a bunk bed and then there I was on the top bunk nodding off to sleep.

The first thing I can recall after this was being at the beach with other kids that seemed to be small like me, although to be honest, I didn't really care much about anything, but I do remember that I felt alone and isolated, different in some way but not knowing why.

Thinking back, I never really thought about mummy or daddy or anything like that. It seemed that I was always moving from one place to the other, with different people feeding me and putting me to bed.

The first time I became aware of my surroundings was at the home of Mrs. D to those who knew her. She lived with her husband in one of those traditionally large Victorian-type houses that you now see being bought by landlords who divide them into separate flats to rent out. When I walked in, I remember noticing this huge suitcase on the right that had just ascended into the abyss, and in front of me was a long passageway that led into a dining room and then into the back kitchen area.

Also, I noticed that I was not the only one to be led into the house; I was with a girl who, at the time, appeared to be much older than me. I came to realise that this girl was my sister, she was only a year older, and we had been together in care every step of the way, we had never been separated from each other, but I suppose at the time, I was just too young to notice.

Life with Mrs. D felt probably the longest that we had stayed anywhere. It was while staying there that I had a strange experience. One night whilst in bed, I felt something unusual near the bottom end of the mattress; it felt almost like pressure near to where my feet were stretched out, it seemed to press down as though someone was sitting there, and for a young child of about 6 years old it was frightening, I remember feeling terrified and throwing my blanket over my head then I started rocking myself from side to side like mad until I must have fallen asleep. For a long time and way into my adulthood, I continued to find comfort in rocking myself to sleep. The next time I was to have that similar eerie experience again would be years later as an adult, and by then, I had found comfort in it because, for no apparent reason, I believed that it was the presence of my mother around me.

We stayed with Mrs. D for a year before we were on the march again, spending some time in children's homes and with other foster carers. It had become a routine with whoever was looking after us that when the social worker was visiting, we always had to dress up that little bit more presentably as if to show that we were being well looked after. The social worker dealing with our case would pop in, ask us a couple of questions like are we ok and what have we been doing and so on, then a quick chat to the foster parents before saying their goodbyes, or they would just pop by, and we would be collected and taken to our next destination, which on this occasion happened to be with the Williams.

Mr. and Mrs. Williams stood at the door and welcomed us in. I was surprised that they already had children of their own that were younger than us, 3 of them. I guess that in those days, having a spare room was not that important. I bunked in, sharing a spacious room with the 2 brothers, and my sister shared with their daughter. Sometime after, Mr. Williams's son from a previous relationship also came to live with us, which made a count of 6 of us kids sharing 2 rooms.

I was around 7 when I moved in with the Williams and thinking back then, I had come to terms with the fact that having a mummy and daddy of my own wasn't a privilege that I was meant to have. What made it easier was that the Williams kids didn't call their parents mum or dad; they called them by their first name, and so did I.

Then something happened that came as a total surprise. My sister and I were called to one side by the Williams and told that our father was coming to visit later that day. Now I remember thinking, "Whose coming" and then thinking, "I have a dad" now, this seemed to excite the rest of the children, who managed to listen in on what was said, and I suppose it was that what made me excited too. But you know, when I think back, I never really noticed how my sister felt about it.

When my father arrived, I remember that I just did not know what to do; I just stood there looking at this stranger and being honest; the rest was just a blur to me because the next thing I remember was waving goodbye as he left. It was then that I remember feeling that I was never going to see him again. I was 8 years old.

Life with the Williams continued, and it became obvious to me that this was going to be a permanent stay.

Whilst in primary school, I was lucky to have the opportunity to go on a camping trip for the week. As one would expect, I was excited about it and found it hard to sleep the night before. In the morning, I arrived at school and got ready to board the coach for the journey. The coach ride there was manic with kids singing and laughing and all sorts. When we arrived at the site, we all got off and huddled around the side of the coach by the baggage compartment to collect our cases. I remember remarking to someone about the size of their case, and then that seemed to trigger a moment of madness for the hyperactive kids who all ran towards me for what we called in those days a pile-on. This is when everyone decides to jump on an individual forming a human layer flattening whoever happens to be underneath, who unfortunately was poor me at the bottom of it. I was bent over and trapped with what felt like a 100-ton weight on my back. It was when everybody finally jumped off me that I realised that I was not able to move my body. I was bent over, literally paralyzed and struggling for air, and I don't even think that anyone had noticed. For that brief moment, I was in trouble. Then out of nowhere, I felt the gentleness of hands wrapped around me, and then, with care and precision, my body was slowly straightened up into an upright position. I began to recover my breath and be aware of my surroundings. Whilst still in pain. I was able to look around, and I saw that all the other kids were away from me and completely oblivious to what had just happened, and even more surprising was that all the staff were with the other kids. No one was with me. I did not see who it was that had helped me even during the holiday as I was still silently suffering with pain; no one came to ask me if I was ok from my ordeal. Today I have come to realise that my guardian angel intervened in recovering me from what could have possibly put me in a wheelchair for the rest of my life, and for that, I am giving out a thank you to my guardian angel.

Time continued and as soon as I knew it, I was 19 and going on my own. I managed to get one-bedroomed rented accommodation from the Council and had scrounged enough household stuff from friends to get by. My sister had also moved out of the Williams and headed south to London for her adventures.

Living on my own had its ups and downs; there were periods when I was unemployed, and on one of those particular days during a very cold winter spell, I found myself with no money. I had almost run out of credit tokens for the gas and electric meters, and with only half a loaf of bread and a packet of custard cream biscuits left to last me till my next social security payment cheque, which wasn't due for days, I was at rock bottom. It got so bad that I felt myself falling into depression. I was sitting on my sofa bed with a quilt wrapped around me because I had turned the heating right down to reserve what little gas I had left. Yet it was still cold enough for me to just about see my breath. I was shivering uncontrollably, thinking about what am I going to do and how am I going to get food, and saying quietly under my breath, I need help. Then just at that moment, there was a knock at the door, still with the quilt wrapped around me and looking through the peephole I could see that it was the older brother of a close friend of mine, which I thought was strange because he was not one who I would expect to pop over and see me for a chat. I invited him in, apologising for the coldness of the place. He sat down and continued by telling me that he was in a bit of a pickle and that he had been let down by a friend as they were both supposed to be starting a job that involved demolishing the basement area of an old nightclub and they were due to start the next morning, and as he was desperate, his brother had suggested me. He didn't need to ask me twice. I believe that if you need help in moments of despair and you ask for help, it will come as it did for me that day.

I spent 10 years in that flat, during which I went through a short relationship resulting in the uncomfortable decision to terminate a pregnancy, something I sorely regret. I have never forgotten that decision, and today I feel that we would have had a beautiful grown-up daughter.

Much later and before I met my wife, I was to make the same decision again, but this time it was the right one; although we did not stay together, we had a son.

When I moved on from my flat, my world changed completely. I had various jobs, I did a bit of travelling, I lived in one place then another until I finally ended up where I first started in a bedroomed Council flat, still single, but was happy, and this is where I met my wife while I was on a night out in Liverpool with friends. I wasn't in the mood for socialising even though I had been convinced to go out. I recall just being content to stand at the bar and watch the night go by. Then out of nowhere, someone appeared right next to me and gently asked if I wanted a drink; when I turned around, there she was, glowing and radiant, and I felt instantly attracted to her. She tells me now that she had seen me earlier and had eventually plucked up the courage to approach me and not knowing why but feel compelled to do so. That was one of the best moments in my life.

We have children now, but it came at a price as we lost our first before gaining 2 wonderful souls who make our lives complete. Because we had children, we were able to get a rented property with a housing association; it was a new build, and we were very excited and grateful to be moving out of what was a very small flat. It was about 2 months later, while in our new home when I got a call from my wife informing me that we had been broken into, which came as a shock but to be honest, it wasn't the first time this had happened to me. I had already been burgled before when I was in my first flat, but I managed to track down the culprit and retrieve my possessions. Unfortunately, no such luck this time.

Time passed, and someone had mentioned to my wife that there was a lady who was a clairvoyant, and if she was interested in having a reading from her, it was agreed. The whole experience was wonderful, and the reading brought up some interesting facts about things that had happened in the past and future events to come. Having the experience of that was what started my wife's interest in spirituality, and over the next few years, she attended spiritual circles and healing classes.

My wife came home from one of her regular circle meetings and said that she had a vision in her meditation that was significant to my father. It had been many years since I had thought of him, and in my mind, I had Shut him out and thrown away the key, especially after I had managed to get information about my mother's situation. My sister and I had asked for the records of our time spent in care to be submitted to us. This revealed that our mother had died at an early age of 29 years resulting from compilations due to an operation to remove a lump on her neck; as a result, our father was not in the position to look after us, and there were no other family members, so we were put in care, and with the feeling of abandonment you could say what I felt for my father was not one of love and joy.

So now my wife has mentioned him as significant and knowing what she has told me about spiritual matters, I saw it to be a message and felt that I needed to pursue it.

Unfortunately, all efforts to locate him failed; both my sister and I didn't have much to go on, just information from our birth certificate and information that we had acquired from our mother's death certificate, plus some extracts from our care records, but nothing else. He did have an unpopular middle name that I thought could be an advantage in narrowing him down. We even tried a private agency that specialised in people searches, but that came back negative, so we gave up the search, and after a while, the thought of looking for him became a distant memory.

As time went by, my wife and I made the decision to move home, and that is when I decided that I would join a spiritual circle to see what it was all about, and I must confess that it was the best decision that I have ever made.

I attended many times in different places, and it wasn't what I had expected at all, certainly not like what they used to put on the telly in those days when they portrayed these things as being spooky and scary. Actually, it's the opposite, with everyone being friendly and warm, and I remember thinking how surprisingly widespread this is with so many people open to spirituality. People of all walks of life too, some looking for answers or just wanting to learn, it doesn't matter if you are wealthy or poor, or what religion you are in or what colour you are, this is for everyone. This experience has taught me a lot about myself and how I see life in all living things and that we are all on a journey, a path if you like, towards our life's purpose.

It was during a spiritual workshop that I opened myself up to forgiveness towards the ill feelings I had for my father and promised that if I was ever to see him again in this life or in spirit, I would wrap my arms around him and tell him that I love him, it was an emotional experience, and it felt like a huge weight had been lifted from my shoulders, I felt free from hate, not just for my father but for everybody.

By now, I was working in IT and shared an office with 2 other professionals. It was a small office with the only window looking into a smaller room space next to where the main computer-type devices lived and what we called the server room. Now and again, I would look through the window at the flashing green lights and the spaghetti of cables connected to the networked socket emanating from there. Green lights were always a good sight as it meant that all was OK. Our office was always warm, and occasionally during the summer periods, we would open the door to the server room as there were 2 large air-con units inside that turned that room into a fridge, and with the door open, it would give us some cool relief.

One morning not long after settling in at my desk, I noticed several red lights flashing from the server room; my fears were confirmed when I logged on to one of the servers. There was a major issue that needed attention. I informed one of my colleagues that I needed to go into the server room to manually fix the issue. He opened the door, making sure that it was left wide open just in case I needed assistance. I must admit that I was having a difficult time fixing the problem, my focus was on getting this sorted, and I could hear myself asking for help. "please, I need some help with this" my colleague must have felt that I was in need because I could hear him come into the server room and stand next to me, I was concentrating so much that I just ignored him, but he didn't say anything he just stood there looking at what I was trying to do. Then within 30 seconds, I had sussed out what was causing the issue, and to my delight, I managed to resolve it. I turned to my colleague to speak to him, and he had gone. Now that was strange because he was just standing right next to me. I could see his shadow. I hurried into the office to see if he had gone to his seat, but there was no one in the office; there was just silence. From that moment, I knew that I had been given the help I had asked for.

Many months later, while on my computer, I had it in my head to type in my dad's name in the search engine. This is something that I had done 100 times over the years without results, so it was just another routine task that I tortured myself through, knowing I wasn't going to get anywhere. What did happen, though, was that I had stumbled on a site that offered to find lost relatives in America. I never thought of looking there for him, but because the information was free, I continued. I put his full name and estimated details in, and it came up with 3 possible names and addresses and even with dates of birth included, one of which did appear realistic. I discussed it with my sister, and we both decided to forward the information to the Salvation Army as they have a people finder unit for family members. So along with all the information that we held, we provided enough details required for them to start an investigation. We had done something like this before and had even written a letter to an address that was found on a UK people search website using the electoral roll information, but the letter came back saying it was not him, so on this occasion, we didn't have our hopes up, it was just another shot in the dark attempt.

Every morning I got up in time to be at the bus stop by 6:45 am, and on this occasion, I was waiting alone under the morning sun and gazing sharply ahead in the distance for any indication of movement that resembled a big red bus. Then a bright white feather floated right in front of me. It was so close it almost touched my nose as it gently settled on the sidewalk between my feet. I have been told that feathers are a sign from the angels as a reminder that they are all about us to help us in time of need. I bent down, picked it up, and put it in my pocket, and as I did so, I had a feeling of warmth and protection, and I was ready to face whatever the day had installed for me.

Time continued to pass, and I received a phone call from the Salvation Army. It was the case worker who was leading the search for my father. She said that she had good news for me and that my father had been found, they had been in contact with him, and he was excited to talk to us.

The news sent a bolt of excitement through my body; I was overwhelmed with joy and immediately contacted my wife and sister, who received the news with the same emotion. The caseworker had given me his phone number, and I spent some time working out what I was going to say to him. I needed to compose myself, ready to make the call. I picked up the phone, and as I started the call, I could feel my heart racing, and I felt excited and nervous at the same time. The phone rang and rang and then I heard him say hello and as I said hello back he cried out "Son is that you"...

One year later and we are finally going to get to meet him face to face, and he will be greeted with arms open wide and love in our hearts.

My journey continues, and I feel that I have more to learn in life; after nearly 50 years of waiting, at least I can say that this part of my path can finally be closed. I thank God for giving me life and helping me to try and understand who I am and that as strange as it may be, experiencing bad times are just as important as enjoying the good times too.

Chapter 3

<u>Mary</u>

I am one of 6 sisters, 2 older and 3 younger, so I guess you could say that makes me the middle one! I am very lucky to be close to all my sisters, and we have a very strong bond, and we have all had different spiritual experiences at some point. I have always been interested in spirituality but never did anything about it.

When I was 15 years old, and on my way home from work, I was walking home when my younger sister came running up to me. She told me my Dad had passed away; surely this couldn't be as he was only 45 years old. I ran into the house, where I found my 2 Aunts (Dad's sisters) waiting for me. It was true my Dad had died; he had a massive heart attack. I started crying, wondering how my Mom was going to cope. My youngest sister was only 1 year old. Somehow Mom found the strength to carry on. We all helped the best we could; I will never forget the day of the funeral; the front garden was full of beautiful flowers and tributes to Dad. Lots of relatives and friends all say their goodbyes.

It was very difficult at times, but somehow we managed to move on with our lives. Mom decided she needed to move house, so we moved to the other side of town.

I started dating when I was about 16, and he was 17; we dated for over 2 years and then decided to get married. We had a lovely white wedding in a church with 3 of my sisters and his sister as bridesmaids. We lived with Mom for a while, and then I found out I was pregnant and gave birth to a lovely baby boy. We managed to get a high-rise flat not far from Mom. We were there for a while when my husband joined the Police force. We were given a Police house, and I found out I was pregnant again (new bricks, new chicks) and gave birth to a beautiful baby girl. My family was complete.

Life was busy, and time flew by. We had to move house again as my husband changed his job. We bought a 3 bedroomed house and made it a lovely home, and we lived here for quite a few years, where our children grew up and left home to start their own independent lives.

Over the years, I came to realise my husband wasn't the man I married, and I suffered a lot of mental abuse. I felt I was always walking on eggshells trying to keep the peace. He could be very moody and not talk to me for weeks. Eventually, we got divorced, it was a very traumatic time, and I felt my whole world was falling apart. I did a lot of crying and wondering where I went wrong. I had no choice but to sell my lovely house. Also, I had to have my poor dog put to sleep. I moved in with my younger sister, who had 2 children, a boy, and a girl. Her daughter was only a baby at the time, so I had her room. Being with my sister's little family helped me a lot. Sometimes I would stay with my daughter, who has given me 2 lovely grandchildren, a boy, and a girl, and I love being with them as they help me to take my mind off things.

My grandchildren, nephew, and niece, have grown up to be lovely young adults. My niece was growing up fast and needed her bedroom back. The council offered me a one-bedroomed low-rise flat, and my brother-in-law decorated it for me. I moved in and made it nice and homely, but I was never really happy there. I had been in the flat about 3 years when I got talking to a neighbour who asked me out. I suddenly felt good again and accepted. We seemed to get on well and were together for a few years and had some good times. I noticed he couldn't seem to do without a drink, and he became very possessive and controlling. I felt trapped and very uneasy as he was worse when he had one drink too many. I knew I had to end this relationship, and he didn't take it very well. Once again, I was on my own, but I had really good friends who encouraged me to get on with my life.

I had always felt something was missing from my life, and one day I heard about an Evening of Mediumship for Help the Hero's, a charity night. As I said earlier, I am very interested in this sort of thing and asked a friend if she would come along with me and I had a reading. The Medium I saw told me I had a sixth sense and also healing hands. I knew I had something as I had always picked up things that might happen but never thought I would pursue them.

I was told to speak to Louise as she was thinking of starting a beginner's spiritual awareness circle, but she was doing readings at the time, so I was unable to speak to her. As we were leaving, I spoke to her husband, and we joked about the bottles of wine (raffle prizes). I left my phone number, and we went home. The next day Louise called to say my friend and I had won a bottle of wine each. We had a chat about the medium evening, and she told me she was starting a beginner's awareness spiritual circle; I said I would be interested, and she asked if I would like to come along, which I did. There were about 12 ladies on the Tuesday evening course, and we all got along really well.

We did exercises to open up our third eye to see what visions we could get for each other. I enjoyed the experience immensely also, the calmness that I hadn't felt for a long time. We met every Tuesday, and I was slowly progressing. I started to notice that my hands were getting hot, so I spoke to Louise about this, and she asked if I would like to do a Reiki 1 and 2 attunement course. I decided to do this, which took about 6 months, the energy was amazing, and I loved it. I feel it gave me a new perspective on my life, and I have made new friends.

I was on my way out one night when I fell down the stairs, badly spraining my ankle; after this, I found the stairs a struggle. Also, I had heart problems. I prayed to the Angels to find me somewhere else to live where I could be happy and not far from my family and friends. I even told The Council I would like a Bungalow (well, if you don't ask, you don't get it.) I kept praying and trying to stay positive. I decided to ask my Doctor to supply me with a letter supporting my application to give to the Council explaining my health issues. When I got the letter, I handed it to the Council and awaited their reply. I received a letter saying they were sending someone to assess me. A nice lady came and could see I was struggling after she asked a few questions; she said she would be in touch. I prayed again and again, and after a few weeks, when I was just about to give up, I received a letter asking me if I would like to view a bungalow. Arrangements were made, and I asked Louise if she would come with me, and she did. When we pulled up at the car park, she said what a lovely area, and I didn't even know these bungalows existed. I had driven past a few times the ambience was lovely. The lady from the Council arrived with the keys, and we went inside and had a good look around. A lot of work was needed (but then most places do); I just needed to put my stamp on it. I asked my brother-in-law to decorate it for me, and I accepted the keys. I moved in, and it is very peaceful and tranquil. I love it here. I truly believe the Angels answered my prayers. Whilst I have been living here, I have learned the last person to have lived here was a spiritual medium. Angels work in mysterious ways, I think.

One day my clairvoyant sister visited and said I am not alone here. There is a cat that comes and sits on your lap, and I have been told the same thing by someone else. How lovely is that as I don't have any pets? I had been here a few years when the bungalow next door became available. After a few weeks, I noticed someone who I recognised viewing it; she was a friend of mine who I hadn't seen for a while, but I had heard she was looking for somewhere else to live. She also is a Medium and a very spiritual lady; again, the Angels are working their magic. I feel blessed to have like-minded people around. I have also taken my Reiki healing to another level. I am now a Reiki Master and do healing on friends and family who say I am like a powerhouse as my hands get very hot. I am also drawn to crystals and sometimes use them when I am doing a healing session.

It is hard to believe how things have changed for me. Life has its ups and downs, but thanks to my family and friends and especially the Angels, I have more ups than downs. Sometimes when things are falling apart, they may be falling into place. Where there is hope, there is faith, and where there is faith, miracles happen.

Chapter 4

Dee

I think I was always meant to be working spiritually as when I was young, my Mom and Nan believed in mediumship and used to say they were going to see the spooks. I remember on one occasion, I was taken by my Mom to a spiritual healer who laid his hands on my shoulder; at the time, I didn't know what was happening. However, later on, my Mom used to talk about it, but I didn't do anything with the spiritual side of my life until I was a manager of a bookies shop and a lady named Louise came to work with us, and she used to read palms in between taking bets, setting bets and marking the board – wonderful chaos.

I started to feel as if I was picking different feelings and started to open up to using my sixth sense. One afternoon in the shop and it was unusually quiet. Louise said something was going to happen. "I think a bomb is going to go off somewhere" she could see a big hole where a bomb had exploded. I then felt there was going to be a train crash; the 2 things seemed to come together. That night on the news, there had been a bomb blast. It was the Brighton bombing, and there was also a train crash that day. I was gobsmacked as it was what we had seen in the clairvoyant visions. I decided then to join the meditation circle that Louise went to and met some lovely people and learned about linking with your guides and working clairvoyantly.

On a personal level, I met a partner, Tony, and we got together, and I had a lovely daughter and, 18 months later, a son. Even though I loved Tony, we had a lot of issues and split up. I moved out and went to live in a different area and decided to do a hairdressing course; and worked 3 days a week in a hairdressing shop, and I loved it. I met a friend there and got on really well, we spoke about getting a shop together, and we started looking for premises and found one we could afford. When I worked with Louise, she read in my palm she could see a shop with bottles on shelves around the walls. We thought it was a sweet shop, but of course, it was the new hairdressers we had bought and put all the bottles of shampoos and conditioners around the shelves. Things took a turn for the better with the shop, and I met a lovely man who came into my life, and things changed completely. We got married, and I love him to bits. I call him my toy boy as he is a bit younger than me.

I didn't see much of Louise through all the changes. However, there were problems with the shop, and we decided to split the shop, and I moved away to a new house in a different area which I love. It has a large garage on the front, so we decided to turn it into a hairdressing salon where I could have clients come, and it took off very well.

I felt drawn to go and see Louise for reading, and at this time, she was doing some Reiki attunement days and asked me if I ever wanted to learn about healing to give her a ring. I started to think about it and felt very drawn to learning about Reiki. I attended the Reiki 1 attunement day and loved it. I opened up to the amazing energy and knew it was my pathway; later on, I completed Reiki 2 and also the Reiki masters, and it brought such a lot of lovely energy and upliftment into my life.

Also, at this reading, Louise asked me if I had looked at another salon with a flat above. She said she could see my daughter coming down the stairs from the flat with a baby in her arms, and she looked about 35 years old. At this time, my daughter didn't have a partner and certainly didn't want any children. Through circumstances with my partner's business, we decided to make office space for him at home, upstairs in the large bedroom. My daughter became involved in the family business and is now 35, and is expecting a baby. We are eagerly waiting for the new arrival and to see her coming down the stairs with a new baby.

I just wanted to help people feel the same and started healing people in my hairdressing salon and became very interested in the lovely packs of angel cards and bought a pack. I started sitting back in a circle with Louise doing meditation, feeling my guides, angels, and clairvoyance, moving close to bringing the visions of clairvoyance through. As I completed my Reiki master's, I started to attune people to this wonderful therapy. I now feel this is my calling in life.

My clairvoyance and working with the angel cards have enhanced my life and have also helped a lot of people with Angel guidance. We never know where life will take us.

Chapter 5

Jessie

Born into a working-class family who believed children should be seen and not heard and were not used to expressing affection, praise or encouragement, I grew up timid with low self-esteem. Discipline was given by way of a cane, which was stored in the sink unit cupboard, across the back of my legs if I was naughty or 'played up'. I don't ever recall my sister 4 ½ years younger than me, receiving the punishment, though. Perhaps my parents thought she was always good. When she came on the scene, I felt more unloved than ever as she was fussed over by my parents, family, and friends.

In the school holidays, while dad was at work, mum would leave me home alone while she took my sister out in the pram, I think mainly to the shops. I used to be terrified being in the house on my own in case this 'boggy man' the adults warned me about would come and get me. If mum had gone out before I woke, I would climb into my sister's cot and hide under the covers, or if mum went out after I got up, I would lock myself into the kitchen. If I needed the toilet, I did it in the washing-up bowl and climbed on a chair to open the window and tip it outside. I was just too scared to go through the house to the bathroom.

From when I was about 7 till I was about 10, I used to pretend I had an elder brother who I used to play with. One day I asked my mum what would she have named me if I had been a boy; she seemed startled but answered Ian. Several mediums since I have been on my spiritual path have said I have an elder brother in spirit yet hadn't known this experience I had as a child. I expect mum had a miscarriage before she had me. But in those days, things like that were swept under the carpet' and never mentioned.

As my sister got older, she got wise to the fact that my parents would believe her over me and often made trouble for me by lying to them that I'd hit her or take something from her. Once when we were at my aunt's, and I was outside the bathroom door waiting for my mum to finish with the toilet, my sister came and stood in front of me; I told her I was next, that I'd been waiting some time, but she pushed me and made a commotion and whined to my aunt who came to see what was happening and when my mum came out of the bathroom my sister told her that I was pushing in front of her. Of course, they believed her, and she was allowed in the bathroom before me, smiling to herself.

At school, I would do what anyone told me to, whether it be the teachers or my peers. At infant school, one girl told me she knew I had taken money out of her coat pocket, I told her I hadn't, which was true, but she said she would tell the teacher I had and I would be in serious trouble. If I paid her back, she wouldn't say anything. So there I was, giving her my pocket money every week. It went on for months, but I was too scared to say anything; who would believe me?

I was bullied in junior school and senior school. Once I had a bike, a second-hand one my parents gave me for my birthday, I would skip some of the afternoons at senior school to escape the misery of teachers picking on me and my peers calling me names and looking down on me; they even laughed at my bike as they had new bikes. I would ride around streets not too near home and go home when it was time as if I'd been at school so mum wouldn't suspect.

As a teenager, I was so shy I would blush if a boy sat next to me on the bus. I did have one friend who was in my class, and I would go around with her and her friend who was in another class. That did help my morale somewhat. We went on walks or to the disco.

I wanted to stay on at school though an extra year and go onto Art College as you had to be 16 to start there, I had found out. I dreamt of becoming a dress designer but would settle for being a window dresser or even a tracer as I didn't think I was very clever. But my parents wouldn't hear of it and would mock me in front of my sister. I had to leave school at 15, go into a job, and that was that.

I didn't like my first job working on a printing machine for a research company making brochures and occasionally photographing broken metal parts and developing in a dark room. That part was ok, but I didn't like the main part of the job, the printing and putting the pages in order and stapling. They told me I wasn't working fast enough. So I left after 5 months. In those days, jobs were plentiful, and one could easily find another.

My next job was working in an art shop in the centre of a City which I thought would be suitable for me, but all the dusting of the art pieces every morning and the boredom of standing around waiting for customers as I was given the job of being downstairs in the basement where it was just greeting cards and artists materials. Most of the customers were upstairs looking for paintings and works of art etc. Also, the job entailed working 5 and a half days a week, including Saturdays, so I couldn't see my friends on Saturdays as I had done previously.

While I was at this job, my mum got breast cancer at the age of 39 and died 3 months later at home. I was 16 years old. I was devastated; despite how she treated me, I did love her.

While she was ill, I changed jobs and went to work in an office as a clerk. They sent me on a day release each week to college, where I learned to type, and when I passed the exams, I moved to another department at the office that involved typing.

I did all the housework, washing and ironing, and some gardening for Dad, my sister, and myself. I tried doing the food shopping and cooking at first but wasn't very good at it, so Dad took over taking my sister with him shopping, and he did the cooking. She wasn't asked to help me with the other chores, though; I suppose as she was only 12, I held down a full-time job, having left school at 15 and would go to discos three times a week with my friends.

The following year I met Paul two weeks after my 17th birthday at a local disco. My friend Sandra was meeting her new boyfriend; she'd met him at work there and asked him if he'd bring a mate for me. I didn't like Paul much at; first; I thought him too shy and a little posh. Dad was already going out to a singles club, and he met Lily. A lady with two daughters lived in a council house. He brought her round to our house, but I found it too distressing and could not accept her. I was still grieving for mum. It was only 9 months after mum had passed away. How could dad think of having another woman take mum's place? My sister, on the other hand, seemed to like her and accepted her straight away.

I moved out when I found a bedsit near work. Paul had a car, so he would drive over to see me 3 nights a week and take me over to his parents, where he lived Saturday nights and Sundays. I found comfort with his family; they talked & listened to me.

One evening after work Dad came to see me at my bedsit to tell me that he and Lesley were getting married (only two years after Mum had passed). He didn't ask me to the wedding, so I kept away, not that I knew where it was taking place anyway.

Paul and I married a couple of years later. I asked dad to give me away at the wedding and asked my sister and a cousin to be bridesmaids. I didn't ask Lesley as I didn't want her to take my mum's place in the photos and besides I hadn't been asked to her wedding to my dad.

A couple of years after getting married, I would get the odd premonition either in dreams or any time of the day. Mostly small things such as seeing a particular colour of a ball of wool in my mind and a wool shop then some months later I would find myself buying that colour wool and knitting myself a jumper. One day when walking home from work, I passed a zebra crossing. I suddenly had a vision come into my mind of being hit by a car, being tossed into the air, and crashing down onto the tarmac. I thought it was a warning to be careful, but very soon after, my dad got in touch with me to tell me my sister had been hit by a car on her way home from work on a zebra crossing. Another time I was washing up at the kitchen sink when a vision came to my mind of a fire in the house next door, and it was causing fire damage in my kitchen, which was attached. Later that week, a similar type of house around the corner had a kitchen fire, and the fire brigade came to put it out. The owner had left a chip pan heating on the cooker and forgot about it.

The premonitions didn't happen very often after I had my sons. Although when I was in hospital after having my first son, I had a vision of a fire at the hospital. The feelings I had with the vision were so strong that I packed my belongings in anticipation, and sure enough, there was a fire somewhere in the hospital later (that day or the next, I can't remember now). We were all evacuated from the wards.

When I was expecting my second child (in the days before, you could be told the sex of your baby while pregnant), I so was sure it was going to be a boy that I bought baby boy announcement cards

Before going to a hospital, and of course, I did have a boy.

I didn't get many premonitions after I had my boys, probably because all my energy went into looking after my family and keeping in touch with family and friends. By this time, my stepmother and I were very friendly, and I would go to see her and my dad every week. (Dad and Lesley had visited me before I had my family to ask me to help my sister by taking her out to some dances etc. where she could meet people as she hadn't much of social life and I obliged them and my sister met her future husband when I took her to dance). I doted on my boys, wanting them to feel loved, do well at school, go to any activities outside school they were interested in, and have every chance to fulfil their potential, as I felt I had been denied all that by my parents.

When we had outgrown our little two-bedroom house and needed to move to a larger house, we needed more income. Paul took on some jewellery outwork to do at home in his spare time; he made rings at work for a manufacturing jeweller. I took on cleaning and caretaking jobs. My return to work in an office was out of the question as we couldn't afford childcare, nor was it convenient for grandparents to look after them, and anyway, I wanted to be with them as much as possible.

One evening when going to lock up the rooms for hire at one of the halls where I was caretaker, I met Louise. She asked me if I'd be interested in going to her meditation and spiritual awareness group. I was intrigued, but I needed to collect my youngest from a church group on that particular day of the week. The more I thought about it, though, the more interested I became, and whenever I saw Louise when I went to lock up, I had questions for her. What did the group do, and could one attract evil or mischievous spirits? Louise assured me that like attracts like. When my son had finished the church group course, I started attending Louise's group once a week with friends of mine I had told. And from the first evening, I loved it. We were taught how to take notice of our inner gut feelings and how to develop our psychic abilities. I was surprised to find I was better at 'knowing' things about people than I thought I would. Also, it was much easier if you 'tuned' into someone you didn't know anything about, then logic couldn't get in the way, and you couldn't be thrown by what you already knew about them. We also learned to meditate and visualize and trust what spirits were showing or telling us and how to understand symbols. I found it all fascinating and looked forward to going each week. My premonitions returned not just as daydreams but also in dreams I had when asleep. I was thirsty for more knowledge and would buy lots of books on the subject. From healing to past lives. From therapies to famous mediums autobiographies.

I started Louise's group in January 2000, and over the years, I learned so much as there were also opportunities to go to various

Mind, Body & Spirit fayres, healing, mediumship, etc., talks, classes, and events.

I've learned Reiki Healing and have qualifications and can give healing. I've also practiced reading angel and tarot cards which I felt drawn to do and can give readings; they are surprisingly accurate. I've always maintained an open mind throughout my learning, and still not sure if the readings I can do are spirits telling me or my natural psychic ability, or maybe a mixture of both. I've studied colour therapy, too, and it's amazing how colours affect us all. I know there is God and many, many angels, and pray to them not only for myself but for others too. When I was learning about Angels, if I started to doubt them at all, I would find a white feather appear from nowhere, such as on my bedroom floor. I've learned there's no such thing as coincidence; everything happens for a reason.

I strongly believe we've all had past lives and have regressed a couple of times, and the past lives I was told of made such a lot of sense and gave me an understanding of why certain things have happened in my life, or I have a particular passion. After training to be a Reiki healer, visions of past lives came to me occasionally in my meditations.

At one meeting, a newcomer told me there was someone close to me in spirit who wanted to apologise and ask for my forgiveness, but they couldn't tell me who it was. A short time later, I had a reading from a very good medium who told me she had my mum in spirit. "She's wringing her hands," the medium said, "She's asking if you'll forgive her; she's so sorry for how she treated you as a child. She realises now it was wrong". I was flabbergasted, but I found it easy to forgive her as she was sorry. I have often felt my mum around me since.

When the boys had grown and were in their last years at school, I was made redundant from the town council as a caretaker and cleaner as they sold the building to developers. So I returned to learn and did an NVQ course in Business Administration, passed the exams, and returned to office work in 2002.

Sadly Paul had bowel cancer at 58 and suffered 4 years before he passed over. I was only 55 years old. It felt like I had just lost mum again. She was often on my mind, and I realise now she was around me, supporting me. It hit me hard. I found it extremely difficult to cope mentally and physically; Paul had done such a lot, the home finances for a start which I hadn't a clue about and had to teach myself, mowing lawns and cutting the hedge, decorating, etc. My eldest son was living miles away after finishing university, and the youngest was in his first year at Warwick University, so I was thrown into living on my own. (My dad passed from cancer when I was 44, my sister and her husband didn't bother seeing me, and neither did my stepsisters and their husbands). I saw my stepmother occasionally, but as neither of us had a car and lived a fair way from each other, it wasn't often. I did have a couple of friends that used to help me if I needed to go somewhere where it was difficult to get to. And another friend used to take me to a big food shop sometimes or for days out in her car. Louise and her husband were very good to me too and other members who sat in a circle with us.

Soon after Paul passed, I awoke suddenly from a dream as it was so vivid and seemed so real. Paul had been knocking at the front door, and I opened it to see him standing there wearing clothes he used to wear when alive. He said, "I'm alright, Jessie Ange", which had been his pet name for me, "I'm alright". Of course, I realised later it wasn't a dream; he was visiting me. I've had numerous dreams of him since.

When at yoga class or going off to sleep a couple of years later, I would get visions of colour and designs. I soon had a desire to do something creative and joined a card craft class where I learned the techniques of making greeting cards. I didn't take to the designs the teacher gave us to do and started designing my own at home, people around me I showed seemed impressed, and soon I was selling them. I found making them very therapeutic and still make and sell them now. So I got to do a job of sorts in the art after all.

It is now 10 years since he passed over, and he doesn't seem to be around me much, but there again, I'm a lot more capable now, and for the last 3 years have been meeting and dating other men looking for another partner to make my life complete once again.

About the same time, I met a woman at church who asked me if I would go on a cruise with her. At first, I said I wasn't sure I could afford it, but then I thought I was still working and by this time receiving my state pension, so why not? We have been on a few cruises together to New York, New England, Canada, Bermuda, and the Caribbean. I never dreamed I would travel the world.

I met Alan two and a half years ago on a dating site. He makes me laugh and feel younger. We have been to some very interesting places on holiday together. Such as Egypt, Cyprus, Vietnam, and Cambodia. We also enjoy rock concerts, country walks, and going around historical places of interest. I am enjoying life and having fun again.

He lives in a different town to me, 25 miles away. I go to stay at his for half the week, then come home to be with my son, get some jobs done and see my friends. At the moment I want to keep my own house although he has talked about me moving in with him. I don't feel ready for this yet, but we'll see what happens.

Chapter 6

Christina

One of the readings I always remember was for a young lady who arrived at my house in a chauffeur-driven car. Everything about her said power, even down to the briefcase and black suit that she was wearing.

I had just started the reading when she stopped me as everything I had told her word for word was what this lady's guides had already told her. This lady was a psychic and had said to her spirit guides if I started the reading with these words, she would know that I was genuine.

In the reading, I told her all about her plans to move her business to New York and that she would make a success in her life, but these were very big decisions. After the reading, she thanked me and went out satisfied.

I didn't discover that I had a calling, as I call it, to work for God.

I didn't realise when I was growing up that I had any special gifts. I was the youngest of 5 girls, my only brother died when he was age 7, and this happened 15 years before I was born. My parents never recovered from losing their only son. I lived in a terrace house, and my Mom was a very loving lady. My Dad was bitter over losing his only son. At school, I was always compared to my 3 older sisters, who were clever for different reasons. I got fed up with being compared and couldn't be bothered to do anything, and I was always bottom of the class.

When I was about 12 years old, we had a new art teacher, and she took me to one side and asked me why didn't I make any effort at school. She was a lovely teacher who wanted to know who I was, and I got on well with her. She encouraged me to go to Art College. I loved sport and went to swimming galas.

When I met my hubby, I was mesmerised by him and believed I had known him before from past life links. We got married and had 3 lovely children.

A friend of mine who came to see me had injured her hand, and it was very swollen and bruised. I held her hand and prayed. After I removed my hands and looked at her hand, which looked pink and completely normal. I just put it down to the Arnica tablet that she had taken for the bruising.

"No," she said, "it was you". Don't be daft. I can't do that; what do you mean I'm a healer? I said to my friend, who then said you are a healer; just look how you have healed my hand.

Well, I was curious, so I went to a Spiritual church on Monday night when the healing service took place. One of the healers listened to my story and said I will put my hands over your head to check your aura. Yes, he said we are short of healers, and you can start next week as you are a healer. This was the start of my healing journey.

I gradually learned so much from linking to my spirit guides and from the many workshops I attended, learning also about myself.

When I was 21, my sister was having a baby, and I dreamt she was going into hospital and would have a baby girl, which she did. When my niece grew up, she came to see me and asked if she would have a family, and I told her she would become pregnant and have a child.

Information about people would come into my mind, and I never asked for this to happen. As in Healing, I asked for God's help to make me a pure channel for the person asking for help. I am a CHANNEL. A pair of hands to give love and Healing, which comes through me and from me. Also, I did see so much detail through my third eye, which overwhelmed me. But instead of Shutting down, I wanted to know why this was happening to me.

In meditation, I saw guides around people and got flashes of past lives with some people. I do believe in reincarnation, and I always have. When we meet people who we feel we have previously known in past lives, we feel a real connection to them. Then when we meet other people, we can't connect to them as we pick up their energy and feel we can't trust them and feel they would let us down.

Also, when working clairvoyantly, we know we are working with the third eye, which is the 6th chakra and is in the centre of your brow. When this opens, this links to the colour purple, which you can see when your eyes are closed. The seventh chakra is above your head, and it is the colour violet, this links to the Spirit world. The first chakra is at your base and is red; 2nd chakra is below your navel, colour orange. 3rd chakra is at your solar plexus, the colour yellow. 4th chakra is at your heart and is green; the 5th chakra is at your throat, colour blue. When your chakras are in balance and open, you can then work spiritually, clairvoyantly, and give Healing. Always remember after working to give thanks and ground your energies.

We are not just flesh and blood; yes, I can sometimes feel when these energy fields are not working, like when someone has a heartache, we are out of balance. Yes, it feels painful; that is why the love of God works as it is a powerful and pure energy. I believe this comes directly from God. Working for God does not mean that I don't have challenges, because I do. When or if my faith becomes tested, I ask myself why I did that and what I can do to make myself stronger to make amends. At the end of the day, we are all here to learn, this is our soul journey, and I do not fear death. Heaven is a wonderful place, I know because I have travelled there twice.

THANK YOU FOR READING MY STORY
LOVE AND LIGHT TO YOUR ALL.

Chapter 7

<u>Dennis</u>

I want to explain when I first met Louise.

It must have been around 2008 when I was working for a supermarket in the maintenance department. I celebrated the New Year at some standing stones on the Clent Hills. My thoughts were that I needed to find out why I was 'weird'. Why can I see things that other people can't? I had bought psychic books that you could collect weekly. I opened them and saw all the different types of divination tools = I Ching – Wild Bird Readings – Tarot – Palm Reading – Horoscopes. Different ones that I had never heard of = Chakras – Auras and suchlike. I saw a Tarot reader in 2005, but I didn't see where he was coming from (ignorance on my part). I am a practical man; things have to go in order. This guy Kris was on about opening doors on my spiritual pathway!!! Anyway, I went into this new age shop I had previously been in a few times but never really knew what I wanted. I picked up some smelly josh sticks and coloured stones (Crystals). The inquiry I was seeking was a palm reader for? In the past, I had contacted people who said they could read palms. There always seemed to be an excuse for me not to go, so it never happened.

Whilst I was working in the supermarket, I saw a Physic Fair advert and asked the lady in the show if she had a number for a palm reader, which she gave me as I had an interest in palm reading. When I got home, I rang the number and left a message. Nearly 3 weeks passed, and I hadn't heard anything, and I didn't want to make a nuisance of myself.

From a child, I had heard and seen things that no one else could. I was called weird and not nice names. However, as I got older, I found I was receiving messages from people in spirit who wanted to talk to their loved ones. I had glimpses of the future regarding disruption in the different countries, war, famine, disease, and no fresh water to drink our lifeblood. Mountains exploding, Volcanos and land disappearing under the sea. All sorts of dreams are being shown the way human beings will end up.

However, Louise got in touch with me, and I managed to book an appointment to see her. When I went to her house, she started to talk about my Dad, who had passed to spirit, and how kind he was. No one ever talked about him. Louise started telling me that I had physic books and I am very spiritual. She then read my palm, I can't remember what she said, but when I left her house, my heart felt different. Louise said she was starting a new circle and invited me to come along. It was at some rooms in Coventry. I went to circle, and there were other ladies and a man, John. We gave ourselves different names so we could remember each other's names easier, Dopey Dora, Dennis the Menace, and others which I can't remember.

We started with meditation, and Louise told us to put our feet on the floor, and I went into a meditation. All my spirit guides came to help me, and it was so beautiful. I heard a voice calling us back, and it was Louise. I opened my eyes, and Louise went around the room asking for people's experiences; when she came to me, I gulped. Yes, it was ok, I caught her eye, and she knew where I had been and what I had seen. We then partnered up with another person, one sitting and the other standing, putting their hands near the body. A lady came to see me, and I put my hands scanning from her head down to her elbows, and her elbows felt different. I carried on down to her feet; when I got to her knees, they felt different too. Louise asked me what I could feel. I was uncertain but said around the elbows and knees felt different. She said she has arthritis in her elbows and has had new knees fitted. This was all new to me. We changed partners, and a lovely lady, Dora, was doing the scanning with her hands, and when they were by my back, Whoosh, I started to fall, and Louise asked if I was alright, and Dora kept on saying she was sorry. I thought it was great. Dora did the same, but I was swaying on my feet. Someone said I was putting it on, but I wasn't. The energy to move someone like that is incredible. I then scanned Dora; her head felt like a barricaded fort; it felt like the pressure was being put around her shoulders; I didn't fully understand as I was new to all this. I felt she had problems around her legs. When I had finished, I told Dora what I found, and she said she was going through a divorce and her ex-partner was putting extreme pressure on her. When I mentioned leg issues, she looked at me very quizzically. We haven't met before, have we? She asked. I said no unless we were in a different universe. She said she had served in the Army. Of course, all that marching re. Leg issues. duh....

We all went back to circle, and Louise took us through an exercise to ground us. Visualising coming through a shower to cleanse us and then saying the Lord's Prayer. We tidied up, and Louise asked me if it was ok. I said yes, but I was buzzing. I had opened up to a world that belonged to my spiritual side. Wow, as I left, I thought I couldn't wait for the next circle. I drove very carefully for a few days, with a smile on my face.

At the next circle meeting, we all sat on chairs and went into meditation. I felt I had to outstretch my arms and have my hands turned upwards. It was as though I was receiving something. I now know it was a lotus flower, and I still had the guides wanting to push forward with messages. I found it quite funny as no one on Mother Earth wanted me, but these guys in the spirit world did. After we came out of the meditation, we began to learn about chakras and the energy that can help us in our bodies to keep well. The evening ended, and we had to close down, and Louise ensured we fully understood how important it was to be properly grounded. Everyone was putting away their chairs and hugging each other. Hmm, not for me. I said my good nights and went to my car.

The next circle felt very different. I think it was springtime, and there seemed to be new energy. We sat in a circle, and Louise said this is your time put your feet on Mother Earth. I still felt like the new boy and thought to myself, I want to take all this in small steps and learn from others. I have this massive thing where I interrupt people, so I just took my time and found learning from different people can guide you on different spiritual pathways.

Next circle, we had a lovely meditation, but I didn't travel very far. Hmm, oh well. At that time, the Planets were forming some kind of magnetic show. (2008) I hadn't a clue. Louise asked us to join with a partner, and we were going to do psychic awareness. I would draw an object, transfer the object to the person opposite, and they would describe what had been drawn. My partner got bits, and then we swapped over. I drew a caravan. When I showed her, she said she was thinking of booking a caravan holiday. Spooky. We did a few other things that night, all to do with psychic awareness. Some people had brought in their Tarot cards, and they were practising the different meanings of who they were partnered up with. When we finished, Louise ensured we were grounded but told me I was not grounded, but I felt ok. She put her hand over my 3rd eye, and I shuddered as I felt a sensation. I heard voices saying he lights had gone dim, then silence. I made my way to my van in deafening silence. I slept well and overslept for my shift at work. I am usually on time.

Over a period of about 3 years, I went to circle. We were all talking about 2012, but I still hadn't got a clue what spiritual people were on about. Golden Gate, the opening of a cosmic portal, the world, and its understanding are starting to be questioned, and people are coming towards the light. In 2011, I completed Reiki Healing courses up to becoming a Reiki Master.

On one occasion, we were asked to bring a photo or piece of jewellery belonging to someone who had passed away. All the objects were put on a tray with pictures face down. I chose a picture, and I was asked to say whether it was male or female; I said female, and it was a picture of a lady sitting in a corner. I said this lady usually sits on something else. Dee said it was a relative of hers, and she didn't like sitting in a wheelchair. I saw a road sign Axe or Max, and Dee said it was someone called Maxine, who was a good friend of hers. Louise encouraged me for any more information; however, the link had gone, or I didn't understand what was being said. I was then shown a building with no mortar between the brickwork; I thought there must be an issue with the estate. I was given a message to look behind a picture on the mantel shelf, but I never received any confirmation regarding this message.

I was given a piece of jewellery and felt the energy of an elderly gentleman who had problems with his head, but I had no idea how he had passed. Louise asked the rest of the group who it belonged to, but no one identified it, and I stepped down from the platform a bit dazed. At the end of the evening, Dora came to me and apologised and told me it was her father's piece of jewellery and she had his photo in her handbag. Well, I thought the mystery was solved. We ended the evening with a grounding meditation Later on, Dora hugged me. The rooms we used went up for sale, so our circle became a bit hit and miss, which was a pity as I was learning about different things.

2013 I was at the Mind Body and Spirit event, and a lady asked me if I wanted 3 cards, and I said no. However, she turned them over and said you are going south. A few days later, I was in the rooms after the meditation, and we were getting ready to leave; a lady said to me are you thinking about going south. I hadn't mentioned the previous comment a few days earlier. At Tesco, a new manager asked if we could have someone looking after the Bristol area. My arm was in the air accepting the offer; I suddenly thought, who put my hand up? I found myself travelling down South; I had a motor home, so I parked it up at a caravan site and travelled from the site daily. I had to pay for the weekly campsite, it was a great adventure, but I realised my money wouldn't last long. I decided that I needed to find something cheaper and found a room to rent in Weston and moved in. After about 3 days, I heard this muttering, and I opened the bedroom door. A lady was walking up and down the hallway chanting got get a job, I need a job. I advised her I had to get up early, and she apologised but said if I didn't get more money, I would lose the house, but I thought not my problem. I stayed there for about 3 weeks. A store manager gave me a bottle of wine, and I decided I would drink it at the weekend. However, I couldn't find it anywhere and went downstairs, and on the drainer was an empty bottle. I asked the lady if she had taken the wine, and she said yes, it was lovely, have you anymore. I was speechless as also I found out she had gone through my writing stuff, and I advised her they are private.

I went out on my own a lot and was recommended to a lady who ran a holistic therapy business where a lot of psychic and spiritual people met. I was invited along one evening as they had a Reiki share. I got complimented on how I carry out my Healing. I remembered back to the time Louise told me to ensure I had insurance, so I took out a policy and renewed it yearly just in case.

When I got back to my rented room, I found my belongings had been moved to another bedroom, and the landlady informed me she had another person for my room. I started to look for another place to live, but it was taking time. The landlady then told me I had to go and that I would get my deposit back when she had sold the property. I was in a daze and found myself outside a friend's house. And I explained the situation, and she said she knows someone who has a room that he sometimes rents out. I went around to see this man, George, and we discussed the rent and deposit, and I moved in about 3 days later. It was a warm day, and I heard lovely guitar music, which I later found out was George, my new landlord.

I have found over time, whilst attending circle with Louise that she has shared her knowledge, and it has been a comfort to me as at the beginning of my spiritual journey, there was so much I didn't understand. I now have become very interested in numerology and have met people through doing courses on this subject and now want to continue and teach this amazing knowledge that can map out what can happen in your life from just your date of birth. At last, I have now found my true spiritual path.

I have never seen Louise flustered; she always says how she feels about a person's situation. I have come to love myself whilst learning from others. I think if I hadn't met Louise, I would have taken a very different path.

Thanks, Louise, you are a beautiful soul, and I am proud to call you my friend. Xx

Chapter 8

<u>June</u>

During the 1980's I had many brushes with cancer, and my best friend also passed away. These difficult times led me on a quest for self-healing, knowledge, and a way of making sense of my life. I was 29 years old.

I asked a neighbour to check the times and days I could go to the local spiritual church for Healing. I have absolutely no idea how I knew Healing took place there.

Off I went and received my first hands-on Healing. The healer said I was probably experiencing karma. So, I came home and looked up the meaning; difficult to think it wasn't an everyday word back then. I was horrified. I took it that it was all my own doing and that I couldn't do anything to change it.

I had been doing a lot of studying, and life had been rather heavy, so I decided to go to 'night school' and learn something, just for fun. Astrology, I was hooked from the first lesson. It was here I met a beautiful soul who happens to be the author of this book. No one like her had ever entered my life before. I clearly remember her calmly walking into a lesson one evening when it was nearly over. She explained there was a lady on the bus who was in trouble; she had never met her before but stayed and talked to her. It was obvious that to Louise, it wasn't a big deal. It was just what you do when there is someone in need.

The classes were incredible. I learned about meditation. How to turn my awareness inwardly and feel the energy of the planets. Align my consciousness with aspects of my birth chart. Heal and change my subconscious processes. I witnessed truly phenomenal occurrences, such as a crystal splitting in half. The group's energy was incredibly powerful.

One evening at our astrology teacher's home where we were meditating. The energy was amazing, and there was a quartz crystal on the table. After we came back from our meditations, the crystal in the middle of the group split into two halves. This was caused by the powerful energies in the room.

At some point, our Astrology teacher held a colour healing workshop at her home. Louise and I both went along. There, I met someone called Jean. We were paired together; she told me I was giving her Healing. I was amazed. I had no idea I could 'do the healing' Then, during the break, she gave me a message from my friend from the spirit world. This was all new to me, and my curiosity, fascination, and desire to learn as much as I could be fully awakened.

I discovered Jean held a circle at her home and, in a rather childlike fashion, said, "Can I come too"?

Weeks passed, and my sister gave birth to my nephew. I went to visit her in hospital. In the next bed was Jean's daughter-in-law. Jean looked at me and said, 'my house next week' and proceeded to give me her address and details of the circle.

I clearly remember driving there; I was so excited. Then I became nervous, wondering what would take place if it were scary. By the time I went inside, I was very anxious. Jean asked what I was concerned about. I could laugh now, but I denied it. Another sitter explained she could see my aura and could interpret it as being worried!!!!! With another new word (aura), my vocabulary was expanded. Louise was also there, sitting in this incredible circle. We were doing rescue work. Helping lost souls who had passed over to find the light and be taken over to the Spirit world. Just to reassure anyone reading this, I was taught about closing down and protection. We all met regularly for a long time.

Louise and I went to a group of Spiritualists and Healers. Held by a lovely couple, Peter and Pauline, in their flat. The meeting was later moved above a social club. Probably not the best place for circle work. We encountered some unusual spirits drawing close; they were often looking for people in the bar! There was a sitter here who used to speak in ancient tongues. Someone recorded it and took it to the language school at the University. It was an ancient form of Hebrew. This group finally moved to a large house where the Spiritualist Church still thrives today.

Chapter 9

<u>Emma</u>

As a small child, I remember being aware of a presence and of being watched and a sense of not being alone.

The first time I remember seeing something, I was about five. I was lying in bed with the door half open, listening to the drone of the TV downstairs, when I felt a prickly sensation at the back of my head and neck; at the same time, I became aware of movement on the landing through my half-opened door. As my eyes became accustomed to the dark, I could see a dark figure creeping down the landing towards my room. I was frozen with fear, too afraid to move or call out and too afraid to take my eyes off it. As it slowly made its way along the landing, I could see it was a dark outline of a man, no features, just black, what I now believe was a shadowy figure. I finally shut my eyes, squeezing them together tightly, wishing with all my might when I opened them, it would be gone, but when I opened them, it had reached my room and was peering around the doorway, dark fingers curling round the edge. I let out a scream and kept screaming until my parents heard me and ran up the stairs to my room. I tried to explain what I had seen through my sobs, gulping down the air through my tears. My parents did their best to comfort me and tried to come up with a reasonable explanation for what I'd seen, but I knew what I'd seen, and despite their reassurances, I knew there was something more in the house.

I had many experiences after that, I would often feel someone sit on the end of my bed, and when I finally mustered the courage to look, I could see the indent on the bed where someone was sitting; I would then feel the bed go up again as they left. This became a regular occurrence, and while I was frightened, I now believe it was someone there to protect me from the shadowy figure who continued to visit me.

One night I heard a loud scratching noise behind my headboard. I froze, my mind whirring trying to work out what it could be. I went to get up to look, but I was frozen; I couldn't move, my body, limbs, not even my head, only my eyes; I was so frightened, why couldn't I move? I felt a presence, and although I couldn't move my head, I could see a dark shadow in the corner of the room...I screamed and screamed again, but no sound came out; I screamed again for all I was worth but nothing, not a sound. I can only describe a feeling of internal panic, not being able to move or make a sound, knowing I was not alone. I closed my eyes and prayed, saying the Lord's Prayer in my head and calling the angels for help. I opened my eyes, and I thanked whatever had helped me sob quietly through fear. I never told my parents. I'd stopped telling them about things that happened a long time ago as they didn't know what to make of it, and I had sensed their frustration and exasperation, so I kept things to myself. I became aware at a very young age of the spirit world.

It was sometime later that I felt slightly vindicated when one night, the whole family was sitting downstairs watching TV when heavy footsteps could be heard upstairs. Everyone's eyes were fixed on the ceiling, eyes wide, and then realising we were all accounted for and there was no one else in the house; my father found something heavy and marched upstairs expecting to find an intruder. He found nothing, and the footsteps were heard many times over the years, and each time they were heard, I felt a little more vindicated.

I grew up in a small village with two older brothers. Our days were filled with climbing trees, building dens, swimming in rivers, and scraping our knees. My parents were loving and hardworking. My Dad had bought the plot of land when I was only a couple of years old, and we would travel out to the countryside every weekend to watch our house grow, brick by brick, where once cows grazed. My Dad would grow vegetables and fruit in the garden, and Mum would pickle or freeze it for the winter. Both my parents had lived through WW2, and they knew the value of fresh food and wasted nothing. Mum would cook everything from scratch, making her pastry and cakes; there was always a meal for anyone who dropped by. I even remember taking tramps home when I was a child and happily watched them woof down one of Mum's hearty breakfasts followed by a hot mug of tea. She would then find them an old coat or jacket. Dads and send them off with a bag of sandwiches and a slice of cake for later.

My Dad knew all the country ways; he knew every animal track and bird's call. He knew the name of every tree and every fish in the river. I was fascinated and enthralled by him and listened to everything he told me. I remember a trail of people coming to the door, usually on a Sunday, to see Dad, and he would do his best to help them. I was so proud that he was my Dad. I had a special connection to him; he had a way of looking at things. He not only taught me about animals, plants and nature but how to listen to my own heart and that no matter what anyone else says, it's important to listen to that inner voice and only do what feels right, even if there's a room full of people telling you different. He taught me the value of honesty and respect and to see the wonder in the smallest flower and creature. Growing up with two brothers in a rural community, he also knew the value of being able to take care of myself, so he taught me how to throw a punch, but that's another story.

I remember the kindness most of all from both my parents.

The day my Dad was diagnosed with cancer, my world stopped; from that moment, my life would never be the same, and my world was forever changed. Selfishly, I couldn't imagine how I would survive in this world without him. I talked to him about everything. He wasn't just my Dad. He was my best friend, my teacher, protector, confidant, and guide. He was everything to me.

Dad had been given just 6 months to live.

The months that followed were full of lengthy, painful hospital visits. I watched as they put huge needles into his back to draw off fluid around his lungs, utterly horrified at what was torture for him and the suffering and pain he endured without complaint. Dad dealt with it all while I was breaking inside. How could he bear it when I couldn't? I couldn't accept the prognosis or the suffering he was going through, so I began searching for anything that might help. I didn't just want to buy us time; I wanted a cure. I met with the doctor in private I offered to donate a lung. I was terrified at the thought of losing a lung but more terrified at losing my Dad. The doctor shook his head and explained that it was in his chest wall, not his lungs; he said there was nothing they could do.

I left the hospital in a daze, my mind already searching for other ways to help. During the following months, I did my Reiki 1 and 2, so I could at least give him some healing while I searched for help. I delved into herbal medicine, bought Native American teas and tinctures made from bark and herbs known for their healing properties, studied Magnet therapy, Nutritional therapy, Echinacea supplements, visited spiritualist churches, and we even took Dad to see a Psychic Surgeon and prayed. Dad went along with everything I came up with mostly because he thought it was helping me rather than him. Eventually, he said Emma, I'll go when I'm ready, not when I'm told, and I'm not ready.

Dad was doing better with this than I was. He went fishing and spent time gardening. He even took a Maths qualification. He was a clever man who had been moved from school to school as a child and never had the chance of proper education, so I think it was something he wanted to do for himself. I went to work, stopping by every day and spending as much time as I could with him. I dreaded every phone call in case it was the one telling me he was gone. Hospital visits and appointments have become a big part of our lives. My brothers lived much further away but came as much as they possibly could and called every day. I didn't sleep well in case I didn't hear the phone and Mum needed me. I was exhausted mentally and emotionally. It was around this time I met my son's father.

There had been a storm, and I'd lost some roof tiles and asked in the local pub if anyone knew anyone locally who wouldn't rip me off. A few nights later, Sid knocked on the door, telling me he was a roofer and would look at my roof. That was a lie right off the bat. He was a commercial roofer for industrial units, not domestic, and hadn't got a clue how to fix my roof, but I didn't find that out until several visits later when he turned up with a bottle of wine and a stupid grin. The truth was it was a distraction from what I was beginning to realise was a battle I couldn't win with my Dad's illness. I was slowly losing my Dad, bit by bit, day by day. It had become all-consuming, researching remedies, taking courses, praying for a miracle. I think it's fair to say at this point in my life, I was at my lowest and most vulnerable, although I didn't realise it at the time. Sid's visits became more regular, and I fell into a lie, the dream of finally being part of a loving relationship. Nothing could have been further from the truth. What he actually brought to me was lies, deceit, heartache, and pain. But God has a plan and what he also gave me was Luke, and actually, looking back, I think that was his only purpose, and if I had to go through all the heartache he had in store for me to get Luke, then it was worth it and then some.

I didn't think my life could get any worse, but Sid was about to prove me wrong.

Dad was on self-medicated morphine in the last few weeks and was in and out of consciousness; even when awake, he was in a daze because of the morphine. On the last day, we were all there, my brothers were home, and we took turns sitting with Dad while he slept. I sat rubbing his feet and telling him about the weather and the garden when suddenly he sat bolt upright, turned and looked at me, smiled, and said Emma, I've got to go now. His eyes were clear and he was aware, there was no sign of the morphine haze that had enfolded him. Our family gathered together to say our goodbyes, kissed him and each other, and he left this Earth surrounded by love.

The following day my brother had to leave for France. He had an important meeting with clients, he wanted to cancel, but we persuaded him to go. He had been there at the right time when we all needed each other, we could keep in touch over the phone, and it was only for a couple of days. The day he was supposed to return from France, we had a very emotional phone call from him. He had missed his flight and was sitting in the airport bar waiting for another flight when he was approached by a Frenchman asking if he'd just had bereavement. My brother asked him how he could know the Frenchman said because your father is standing next to you, and he said he's not on the ground yet!! He went on relaying personal messages and sending Mum cream roses and left saying Dad would stay until after the funeral.

The day of the funeral came. I was desperate to tell Mum was carrying a baby, but how could I? She was reeling from losing the man she had been with since she was 17. I couldn't hold back the hurt, knowing Dad would not be part of my baby's life or see him grow up. What should have been wonderful news shared with excited grandparents had become a secret I had to hold onto and only share when I could no longer disguise it. I had desperately wanted to tell Mum about my baby, but I didn't know how she'd react. Would she be happy and give her something to look forward to, or would she be upset that I was essentially a single Mum and would probably have to find a way of supporting us both, giving her more to worry about? One thing was certain I couldn't hide it forever.

After the initial shock, she took to knitting like mad, and we looked at prams and baby clothes together. This was something we could share, and this would hopefully give us both something positive to look forward to and, in some way, help us to heal and fill the gaping hole that Dad had left.

Sid's reaction was to distance himself, he spent more time at the pub, and he took himself away on holiday with his mates. I had to buy a second-hand cot while he bought himself a new motorbike. He didn't come with me to any baby scans or hospital appointments. I already felt abandoned and alone. If I thought life couldn't get any worse, Sid was about to prove me wrong. One day I had driven out to see him at a motocross practice; I was 8 months pregnant by now, and on the way home, I began feeling pains. I pulled over on the hard shoulder of the motorway, my pains were becoming regular now, and I called him to tell him where I was and that I thought I was in labour and needed help. Call the AA, he said; what do you want me to do and he hung up. A few minutes later, he drove past me without stopping.

The day I was booked in to be induced, he was nowhere to be seen. One of my brothers came with me, so I wasn't alone, for which I was grateful. After being induced twice, it was a white knuckle ride down to the delivery room. Luke entered the world without a sound, I had managed to deliver Luke with only gas and air, so I'd had no drugs that would have suppressed his crying, so even the nurses were surprised. That night when we were on our own, and the noise of the hospital and ward had quietened down, I held him in my bed, and I knew there was someone I would die for, who I would protect with my life and it was him and me, and from that moment my life would change forever.

Mum hadn't been able to come to the hospital until the following day when my brother brought her, she seemed a little frail now, but her eyes lit up when she held her grandson for the first time. The day came for me to go home and I was all packed up, sitting on the bed holding my baby, watching all the other new Mums leave with husbands or boyfriends and excited families. Sid had arranged to pick us up and take us home; I waited patiently for my turn. Sid eventually arrived carrying a motorcycle helmet and leather gloves. You'll have to make your own arrangements to get home. I'm going to a motorbike sale with my mate, but I'll call you later, he announced before walking away, without waiting for a reply leaving two nurses and a midwife with their mouths hanging open. I asked them to watch Luke while I phoned for a taxi from the payphone in the corridor. A few days later, I was home, and Sid called from a beach in Majorca. Despite the fact he wasn't here, he'd found the birth of our son quite stressful and needed a break.

It was around this time I could see Mum wasn't well, she was hiding it well, but I could see she was struggling. We had made plans for me to go back to work, and she would look after Luke, and I'd pay her, but I knew she wasn't well enough, and I couldn't afford to pay for childcare and the mortgage and bills. So I gave up my job of 11 years and set up as a freelance credit controller working from home so I could take care of Luke and be there for Mum and prayed it would be enough.

About 10 months later, Sid finally decided to move in, I had hoped it would help financially, but his money went to the pub and on motorbikes and himself. He was rarely there, disappearing all weekend motorbike scrambling and most nights in the pub. He never made time for us or bonded with Luke despite my encouragement. He would come home drunk in the early hours throwing bottles of wine up the wall and shouting and intimidating. Random women would answer his phone in the early hours laughing at me, telling me he was busy. One night he came home around 4 am., I'd bolted the door, and I could hear him kicking and banging the door, fumbling with keys. I wouldn't open the door and told him to go back to whoever he'd been with till 4 am. A few minutes later, he'd found a spade outside and was smashing his way through the door, screaming obscenities. I ran upstairs with

Luke in my arms and barricaded us in the back room, pushing furniture up against the door. He eventually made his way into the house, and I could hear him stumbling up the stairs, swearing and slurring. He pounded on the door until the drink got the better of him.

Mum's health declined rapidly, and she was in pain; there was by now a visible lump in her chest, and she could no longer hide it. Reluctantly she agreed to see a doctor. Mum had a large cancerous tumour in her chest, and they wanted to operate, but she refused. The truth was she didn't want to be here anymore without Dad. I think secretly, she'd hoped it would take her without anyone finding out. We begged her to have treatment, but she didn't want to be here anymore, and not even the birth of her grandson could keep her here. Almost a year to the day after losing Dad, Mum left this Earth to be with him, leaving us broken and fragmented; I felt like an orphan, lost and alone.

I thought that somehow Sid would take pity on me and realise I needed support, but he saw it as an opportunity to dismantle me further, an opportunity to break me. He continued to come home drunk, but now he was more threatening, he would tell me I was on my own now, and he was going to take my baby away, and I'd never see him again. He didn't want Luke; he just wanted to control me. The day after my mother's funeral, I overheard him and his family talking about their plans for me. They never called me by name; I was Luke's mother or, more often, just her. I felt like I was losing my identity. I was belittled, berated, criticised, and lied about.

They even told Luke I was a nasty person and needed to be punished. They went through my home, throwing out anything they didn't like. Sid's mother even went through my fridge and pantry, throwing out anything she thought Sid wouldn't like. They were making plans for my home, my son, and for me, and I had no say in it. I felt like I was disappearing. I had no voice, no name; I was becoming invisible.

It's hard to say when the tipping point came. It might have been when Sid was shouting at me and threatening me when Luke, still in nappies, stood between us and shouted at him to leave his Mum alone. There was this baby still wearing nappies standing up for me to a huge, intimidating man. Luke was the only soul other than my Dad to ever have stood up for me. I think right there, and then something changed in me. This beautiful little soul was trying to protect me, and I needed to protect him with my life. Right there and then, I knew it was just us. I didn't want him growing up in an environment where he thought this behaviour was acceptable or, worse, normal. This would affect every relationship he would ever have in his life, with his wife and daughters and anyone else coming to that, and I could not allow this to happen. That night I waited for him to fall into a drunken sleep and packed our overnight stuff; I wrapped Luke up against the cold night air and strapped him in the car, and drove to Mum's empty house. It was cold and dark, far from the bright, warm, welcoming house it had been when Mum and Dad were alive. I made us a bed up on the sofa, making use of old blankets and coats to keep us warm, and then the all too familiar footsteps from my childhood could be heard walking around upstairs. There would be no sleeping that night, but I was no longer a child, I had my child to protect, and I would. I would rather be here with whatever it was walking around upstairs than in my own warm, comfortable cottage with that man.

How could I have gotten so low? How was I sleeping on a sofa in a freezing cold house, too frightened to go to my own home? I didn't want Luke to grow up seeing his mother as afraid, weak, and unable to protect and support him.

By the first light of the next day, I had a spark and a plan, and it involved Feng Shui. I drove home to find the house a mess; empty wine bottles were strewn around the floor; time to find my metal. I emptied all his clothes, boots, shoes, and belongings into bin bags and piled them all on the front lawn, then rang him with a weather report. Why do I care what the weather is doing he laughed....because all your stuff is on the front lawn, and it's about to rain, I said and hung up.....and that's when Luke's Mum found her metal and her spark.

Small Embers

There is a moment in everyone's life when you are on your knees when you can't see a way out or even how to take the first step forward. That's the moment you have to find your steel, that little ember inside that looks like it died and gone out forever, but if you blow very gently, it starts to smoke, just a little, then you blow a little harder, and it starts to glow, and now you've got a start. Keep that ember going, keep feeding it and tending it until you see a spark, and the spark becomes a flame, and the flames get bigger and bigger, and then you've got a fire, and eventually an inferno. Right now, I'm stirring the embers, and they are starting to smoke. I'm lucky I have something worth fighting for, and Luke deserves a Mum that will fight for him if not for herself. I'm finding my fire and my steel.

The next few weeks were full of threats, but like most bullies that lose their power when they don't get a reaction, they wane that's all they were. My Feng Shui was throwing his belongings onto the front lawn, and this was the start of me taking my power back. moved all our stuff back into the main bedroom, I changed the locks, and Luke and I started again. The cottage seemed lighter; i was like there was more air even. We baked cookies, binged watched Scooby Doo, read stories, drew pictures, and stopped being scared.

While I'd found some strength, I felt damaged and was afraic of being damaged beyond repair if I got hurt again. I stayed single for the next 11 years focussing on my son. I painted the house and put it on the market, ready to make a new start. Mum's house was still empty, and my brothers had said I could stay there while I was looking for another house if I painted it and kept it on top of the garden. I enrolled Luke into the same village school I'd attended as a four-year-old, and we took our next step.

One day I was in the kitchen washing up, and I could hear Luke chattering away to himself, at least I thought it was to himself but as I listened, I could hear him leaving big gaps in the chatter as if waiting for someone to reply. Then he would burst into fits of giggles and continue his conversation. "Who are you talking to Luke," I asked. "Nanna and Dandant, silly," he said, looking at the chair next to him and smiling. "Where are they?" I asked, looking round. "Right here," he said, opening his arms wide at the space in front of him. He continued to chat with them. He seemed oblivious to the fact I couldn't see them and could only hear one side of a conversation I longed to be a part of. "What are they saying," asked gently. They're asking me about my game, he said without looking up, "but you never met Dandant darling; how do you know it's him" I said. "Yes, I did," he said quickly. "I saw him in heaven before I came down to you!!" Later he would pick out my Dad's photo from a stack of old photos I was going through, telling me that it was Dandant who he would talk to.

We'd only been at Mums a couple of months. I'd painted the house and was working on the garden when I had some heart-sinking and unexpected news. My brothers decided they wanted to sell the house. I couldn't believe I was going to have to move again. I had done the first move almost completely on my own using my Dads old Ford Fiesta and a trailer, and it had taken it out of me the thought of having to pack up and do it all again after only a couple of months filled me with dread, I would have to move Luke again, and he had only just started school. My heart sank; I would need to find somewhere else to live. The hunt for a decent place to live within reach of Luke's school began. I couldn't find anywhere to rent that I could afford close by and wanted to keep Luke in the same village school. He had had enough upheaval; it wasn't fair that he would have to move schools and home again so soon. I trawled round endless houses, most wouldn't let me take the dogs or cat, let alone the old goose I had in the toe, and I couldn't bear to part with them; we'd lost enough already, so I persisted in my search while Luke was at school. Some houses had dampness and mould on the walls and strange smells. Others had creepy landlords that made me feel very uncomfortable; others were too expensive or too far from Luke's school; it was becoming desperate. Then I heard about a house not far from where I'd already moved from; it seemed madness to be moving back to where I'd come from and have to drive past Mum's empty house every day to get him to school, but I didn't have a choice. Wearily I started putting our home back into boxes

Great Oaks

We moved to a lovely cottage called Great Oaks over 10 years ago. I was immediately aware of the energy in the Cottage as soon as I entered. It has a warm, peaceful, welcoming feeling, and visitors often comment on how comfortable they feel here.

The local Vicar used to preach to the farm labourers and their families. I believe positive energy can be built up in areas where prayers, good intentions, and love are offered. I feel these prayers that built up over the years are partly responsible for the energy in the Cottage.

We felt very blessed to be living here and wanted to find a way of sharing its energy, so Great Oak Animal Rescue opened. Over the years, we have taken in and welcomed dogs, ducks, hens, geese, goats, owls, ferrets, doves, bats, pigeons, and tortoises, as well as an assortment of injured wildlife which we care for and then release back into the wild.

My son, Luke, and I have had many spiritual encounters, many before we came to Great Oak. While I feel and sense energies and sometimes see what I can only describe as a shimmering haze like heat coming off a hot road as well as spirit lights, my son has seen full-bodied apparitions and could tell you the colour of their eyes and what they wore.

During our time at Great Oaks, we have seen lots of spirit light and apparitions between us. I believe the orbs come in on a loving, healing vibration and are attracted to the innocence and pure energy of the animals. Animals teach us so much about unconditional love, empathy, and compassion, allowing us to raise our vibration if we let them by operating on the frequency of love and compassion. I have seen little lights and sensed a presence around a baby, hand-reared goats suffering from pneumonia and not expected to make the night but then went on to fully recover. I am often aware of a presence when I am nursing poorly animals and during these times when we sadly lose one due to illness or injury. While this can be heart-breaking, I feel I am being taught that not all animals are meant to be here for a long time and sometimes only stay to teach us the lessons of empathy and compassion or for them to experience love themselves, perhaps for the first time in their lives.

A dog called Angel has attracted light energy and orbs in particular. Angel came to us at a very busy time with a houseful of dogs and a litter of rescue puppies, but as her story of abuse, neglect, and abandonment unfolded over the phone, I felt a presence and knew I couldn't turn her away. She arrived in the most terrible state, painfully thin, covered in urine burns, eyes full of fear. She cowered in fear at every noise, movement, and word. It took some time for her to realise she was safe. By the time a kennel space became available, both she and I knew she was already home and would be staying.

Four years on, she is the kindest of soul, and her beautiful, loving energy attracts orbs and spirit light. She welcomes, nurtures, mothers, and protects any animal that comes through our doors; she has even played Mum to three baby hand-reared goats and a litter of pups that didn't belong to her, even attempting to feed them herself. She stands guard over baby ducklings and chicks and nurtures anything needing a Mum.

There are so many spiritual stories I could share about Great Oaks. One night, for example, I fell asleep on the sofa in front of the fire. A log rolled out of the log burner while I was sleeping and the room filled with smoke. I was woken by a hard slap on my leg but thinking I was dreaming, I fell back to sleep, oblivious to the danger I was in, only to be woken again by an even harder slap and a bright light in the room visible even through the smoke. By this time, the room was so full of smoke I could only see a few inches off the floor; I could barely breathe. I rolled off the sofa onto the floor, coughing and choking on the thick grey wood smoke, my eyes stinging and watering. I crawled into the kitchen.

As soon as I was safe, I looked back into the room, which was now full of smoke from floor to ceiling, and watched the light disappear into the thick grey smoke. I truly believe I would have died that night if it hadn't been for spirit intervention.

I had been to visit friends in Wales and was making my way home, taking my time, taking in the beautiful views as I drove homeward. I reached a single-track mountain road. One side was a sheer vertical wall of mountain rock, the other a sheer drop over the edge into a ravine with no railings or fencing of any sort, no passing places or road widening at all. I took my time hugging the mountain wall as I tried not to look down.

As I reached a sharp bend, a small truck suddenly appeared hurtling towards me at speed just a few yards in front of me, the driver not expecting to see someone on such a remote road. There was nowhere to go, the sheer rock face or the ravine, nothing in between. At that moment, I could see the driver's face and the look of shock and terror on his face as he realised he could not stop in time and neither could I and neither of us had anywhere to go. The ruck was now only a few feet away, so close I could clearly see his eyes; knowing there was no missing me, I saw him close his eyes, waiting for the inevitable impact.

At that moment, the most bizarre thing happened; everything seemed to slow down and go into slow motion. I knew this was it, that there was no way out, and I thought I was going to die, but at that same moment, I became completely overwhelmed by a sense of peace. I closed my eyes, knowing there was no way out; I sank back in my seat and waited for the impact feeling the most beautiful peace and calm.

A few seconds passed..... With no crash.....impossible! I opened my eyes; the track was clear, with no truck in sight! I put on the brakes. Had he driven over the edge into the ravine to avoid me? Surely I'd have heard the crash? I scanned the bottom of the mountain, but nothing! Then I checked the rear view mirror and saw the impossible...... the truck was on the other side of me, facing the way I had come. He, too, had pulled over, no doubt in as much disbelief as I was. This was totally and utterly impossible this was a single track, barely enough room for a car, let alone a small truck with absolutely nowhere and no way of overtaking, and we had both closed our eyes at the moment of impact, which never came and I doubt either of us will ever know why.

I have never shared this with anyone, let alone written it down because I realise how unbelievable it is. I can only think that something miraculous happened that day, and I witnessed a miracle.

Sacred Earth

The Natural World is our bible, we don't have chapters and verses and we have trees, fish, and animals. The creation is the manifestation of energy through matter. Because the Universe is made up of manifestations of energy, the options for those manifestations are infinite, but we have to admit that the way it has manifested itself is organised. It is the most intricate organisation. We don't know how we impact its law; we can only talk about how its law impacts us. We can make no judgement about nature. The Indian sense of natural law is that nature informs us, and it is our obligation to read nature as you would a book, to feel nature as you would a poem, to touch nature as you would yourself, to be a part of that and step into its cycles as much as you can.

(Native American Spirituality) Arthur Versluis.

Animals

I had and still do have a great love and affinity for animals and all creatures, great and small. I also had a strong pull towards anything remotely to do with Native American Indians and their beliefs and culture; it was almost as if I already knew it. I made myself a little cloth medicine bag and filled it with little treasures, shells, acorns, lavender, and anything else I was drawn to. I understood their connection to the Earth and their deep respect for it, in particular their belief that everything has an energy or spirit, the earth, the wind, the rivers, trees, and animals, and they had a deep respect for all these things offering thanks and prayers for the spirit of any animal they killed to feed their families, using every bone, claw, and fibre of it wasting nothing. I grew up with this teaching in my head, even writing some Native American proverbs on my bedroom wall.

When the Earth is sick and the animals begin to disappear, when this happens, the Warriors of the Rainbow will come to save them. One day there will be a time when the Earth has been ravaged and polluted, the forests have been destroyed, the birds will fall from the air, the water will be blackened, the fish being poisoned in the rivers and streams, and the trees will no longer be. Mankind as we know it would cease to exist.

Only when the last fish is caught will we realise we cannot eat money.

We have forgotten how to treat the planet and all other creatures and sentient beings that live upon it with respect. We have forgotten they have as much right to be here as we do. We do not own the sky, the Earth, the water, or the trees, yet we treat everything as commodities to be bought and sold to the highest bidder. I mourn the loss of every tree and every creature; we have lost our connection to the Earth, to each other, and to ourselves. Birds have fallen from the sky due to sound and radio waves, waters have been blackened by massive oil spills, forests and ancient woodlands destroyed to make way for roads and housing, and seas have been polluted by plastic and rubbish, killing its creatures.

Chapter 10

Aimee Jane

I can remember from an early age my Nan talking to me about spiritual things that had happened to her in her life. I loved my Nan and spent a lot of time with her. My 2 brothers were never interested in any of her stories, but I loved them. Also, she could read the tea leaves, which fascinated me.

I remember visiting a healing lodge in Hampshire. A group of us travelled there in a minibus many years ago. We travelled fairly early one Monday morning as we had found out the lodge held a Healing service on Monday afternoons. It was quite a distance to travel, and we needed to ensure we reached there around lunchtime. You had to book in if you wished to have healed, and we weren't sure how popular or busy they would be.

There were beautiful grounds to walk around. The Temple was circular, an outstanding building that really leaves an impression on you; something out of the ordinary, a feeling of knowing, will take place.

The Healers came forward to meet us all ladies wearing blue robes, and there was serenity, peace which you could sense and feel the energy from them. We were taken individually to a room where we gave our details and the reasons why we wanted the Healing. We were put at ease with their air of confidence, kindness, and a feeling of love.

We then proceeded into the Temple, taking our chairs before the Healing Service started. A really beautiful atmosphere in the Temple is just experiencing this; you feel the healing energy, love, peace, and silence. A young man wearing a white robe led the line of healers (the ladies who had taken our details). They moved gracefully to the front, where there was a row of chairs for people who would be having the Healing. The young man sat apart from the chairs higher up on the platform.

I was sitting halfway down the Temple, eagerly watching all that was taking place, which was nothing like I had ever witnessed before and so different from our Healing Circle.

The people were invited to come up to sit on the chairs to receive Healing. I decided to wait to watch the first group of people to see what happened. I had never seen so many healers gathered together, and they started their Healing at the same time and did everything in sync. I was totally mesmerised and wondered how on Earth they worked all together as they did, totally fascinated. As the Healing drew to a close, they all finished together and stepped back, giving patients a few minutes, and they exchanged a few words with them before the patients left their seats.

The next lot of patients were invited to sit on the chairs. As I was travelling to the Temple, I wasn't sure if I was going to partake in the Healing as I was very hesitant. I felt the healing techniques of all the Healers had a very gentle spiritual and caring energy which I found helped me to relax. I decided to walk to the front to receive Healing.

Whilst the Healing was taking place, I had the most amazing experience. I heard the loudest noise, like a crack of lighting, which I thought everyone else must have heard. My eyes were closed, and I sensed/saw the young man come and stand in front of each one of the patients whilst we were receiving Healing. I thought that was strange as I didn't recall it happening before my Healing. It was truly the most amazing experience in which I did not participate happening at all. I left my chair in awe and wonder and went back and sat quietly in my seat. Watching the next lot of Healing, nothing out of the ordinary seemed to happen like what I had experienced.

After the service was over, we left the Temple. I spoke to the friends I had travelled with and told them of my experience, expecting them to say the same, but no one did. I thought the loud noise I heard was in the Temple, but I then realised it was my inner hearing, and this surprised me.

On the journey home, I was trying to assimilate what had happened. I felt it must have been a Spiritual Awakening, but how and why, I had no idea.

I was just starting to discover the 'Open Circle' and Awareness Classes. After this experience, my development started to accelerate. I felt impressed to write, words would come almost too quickly for me to write them all down, and I wrote pages in the beginning. Alas, they have all gone missing, so I have no record of them at all. I still do writing now, Inspired and Channelled.

I was invited into a Closed Home Circle before this, but I had no idea what they were or anything about them. I started to develop my mediumship. I have continued to progress and develop up to this present day. I have never forgotten the experience at The Healing Lodge and feel it was instrumental in getting me started on my spiritual journey as a Healer and Medium.

I sat in an open development circle and started to pick up feelings and visions from the other people in the circle. I couldn't believe I could do anything like this but felt impressed to say what I had seen and felt. I was asked by the church leader if I would like to work on the platform giving out any messages I received from the loved ones in the spirit of the people in the congregation.

I started with an opening prayer which was channelled down to me by my guides. It brought comfort to the people in the congregation who often came up after to speak to me. I then became very drawn to angel pictures and the lovely angel oracle cards. When I looked at them, I felt there was a presence next to me, and I was inspired to write down the words, which were from Archangel Michael and Archangel Raphael. What a privilege and very humbling. From then on, I was inspired to teach the words I had channelled from the angels. I started to do workshops for people who wanted to learn about the Angelic Realms, and I continue to do these lovely workshops today. Also, visit spiritual churches to work on the platforms.

My life has had its ups and downs, but with the help of my guides, helpers, and angels, I have overcome my problems. I am sure my Nan comes and sits with me, and I still have lots of memories of the time we spent together many moons ago.

Chapter 11

<u>Daisy</u>

My spiritual experiences started when I met a wonderful spiritual man Bert. He ran a lovely sanctuary in the South; he also had a psychic artist with him. My first physical proof was watching the artist draw and give a reading to my friend. The picture he drew was my friend's– Nan; the only thing we couldn't connect with was the spectacles as everything else was spot on, the colour of her hair, shape of face and eyes even down to the clothing.

At this time, I spoke to Brian, and he invited me to his sanctuary for a workshop. He believed so much in me that he said he wouldn't charge me and advised me to just come along as he knew I would get so much from the workshop. So a couple of months later, I went a little apprehensive that he wouldn't remember me, but he did and I experienced so much.

I teamed up with a lady there, and we were both given a sheet of paper and were asked to fold or scrunch whatever we felt most comfortable with and then exchange the paper and give each other reading. Well, we were both blown away by what we picked up on each other.

Later that day, we sat in the wee Church that Bert had turned his garage into. He asked me to get up and talk to the group about spirituality or anything else that came to me. I was very nervous and lacking in confidence about getting up in front of about 30 people. However, I managed to overcome my initial fears and started to give out thoughts that came to mind and then realised I was giving messages to the congregation that they connected with. One lady came up to me afterward and couldn't thank me enough.

I have always been interested in the spiritual side from when my aunt took me to a caravan park when I was 17 to have a reading by a gypsy lady. She had me spooked at the time but also intrigued. I have since had many readings and have also given readings myself. I was taught the tea leaves by a family friend, and they still blow me away today at what I get when I look into someone's cup. In my hubby's sister's cup, I saw the passing of their mum and said to his sister that her husband wouldn't be long after, maybe 6 months! She said she wanted more time with her husband as she had looked after her mum so much. I told her that it was her time and her retirement. Also, I saw the letters L & S, which were her daughter and son in laws initials. I predicted they would go through a tough time medically and with their own family. They have since been diagnosed with different ailments, and their daughter has experienced some trouble.

Another physical experience, Table Tilting, was at a spiritual church I attended. Wow, wow. I watched this table start at the other side of the room, and 3 people had their fingertips on it, and it was rocking back, forth, and sideways to move around the room. It stopped a couple of times, and the medium asked if there was a message for the person the table had stopped at. The table lent back, which meant no. I had a really strong feeling that the table was coming to me. Moments later, it stopped by me; the medium asked if I was the person it wanted to connect with. The table lent hard on my legs, and I had a feeling that I wasn't allowed to get up, but I couldn't even if I wanted to. The medium asked questions to the spirit; again, I had a feeling that this wasn't for me but for someone I knew. It was my friend's mum who came through, and my friend was sitting at another table giving messages. We laughed, saying why didn't your mum just go to your table, think she was just giving me more proof. I have since been to the couple's home that does the table tilting events and has been blown away by how much the table moves and only fingertips are on it.

I have learned that spirit moves in so many ways, giving messages in different forms, but most of all, we all have gut instincts and feelings. Believe that most, if not all, of them, are from spirits trying to connect or guide you in some way.

God Bless all xx

Chapter 12

Jack – Louise's Son

My son Jack was very musically minded from an early age, always wanting a guitar. We eventually bought him one when he was about 12 years old. He was always practising and got together with a few lads when he was about 15, and they formed a band. His first gig was in a pub in town, and it was nerve-racking for us, but we loved it. They began to play in different pubs in the area, and we always went to see them perform.

He'd had a couple of relationships that didn't turn out as he had hoped and said he wasn't going to bother again. He started meeting up with his old schoolmates and decided to go to see the Eclipse in 1999 in Cornwall. They arranged to go on a Sunday to look around for the best place to be to see the eclipse, but they had car trouble and ended up going on a Monday instead. They got down to Portsmouth, and when they parked the car to go for a look round, they saw a pub that had just opened that day with free food and a band playing. They went in to get a free meal and, of course, listen to the music. The girl behind the bar started chatting to Jack, and he told her they played in a band, and she asked them if they would like to play a few numbers while the band that was performing had a break. They got up on the stage and started playing lots of Beatles music for a bit of fun as everyone knew the words to their songs. The barmaid came over to chat with Jack and his friends and asked for Jack's phone number, which he gave her. They then went off to look for the best area to see the eclipse.

When he got home, Alice started ringing Jack and said she would like to come and see him for a weekend which he agreed to but didn't seem too bothered. When she came to the house, I started chatting with her, thinking about what a nice person she was. We had lost our lovely cocker spaniel the day before and were all very upset, and she was sympathetic and kind. As the months went on, Jack seemed a lot happier, and as they grew closer, he asked her to move into his flat with him. She moved up a month later and got herself a job in a food restaurant, and met some friends there. She applied for a job in London working for a tour company and got the job, so they decided to move to London.

I was a bit sad to think he was moving away, but everyone has their pathway. They settled into life in London, a faster pace with lots more going on. Jack was still with the band, and his mates said shall we all move to London and see if we can make it there and try to get a record deal.

They all moved and got a flat and loved the life there. Alice's sister came to stay with them and took a liking to the drummer as soon as she saw him. Their romance took off quickly, and when she was going home after being in London for a couple of months, he decided to leave the band and move to the pub in Portsmouth with her. They got married and now have 3 children. Fate had certainly taken a hand here. It was all meant to be.

Alice loved her new job with the tour company taking people around the sites in London. After being there for about 18 months, she rang to say she was expecting a baby, and we were over the moon. 9 months later, our first grandson, Joe, was born, and we couldn't wait to see him 'munch munch' and didn't want to leave when it was time to come home. The week Alice had the baby was a very busy week for us as 6 weeks before this, our daughter, Lucy, had a baby girl, Lily, on a Saturday. My daughter, Vicky, was getting married in the same week, and my lovely Mom fell and broke her hip. We didn't know if we were coming or going. Babies, weddings, and hospitals all in one week, our emotions were all over the place.

When Joe was 3 years old, Alice had a promotion at work and was asked if she would like to go and work abroad in their main office, and she jumped at the chance. So they all moved abroad; I was again sad that my family was moving away and not being able to see my son and his family as often as we would have liked to. However, opportunities come, and you have to take them. Jack and Alice got married abroad, and they had a lovely wedding. We all went over, and of course, they had 2 more lovely grandsons. We have been over numerous times.

Jack's friends who moved to London with him also met girlfriends there. Paul married Julie, and they have 2 sons, and Shaun moved in with his girlfriend for a while, but it didn't work out for him. However, looking at the bigger picture, if Jack hadn't gone to see the eclipse on that Monday, would things have all happened differently? We'll never know if our life is planned out for us.

Chapter 13

<u>Lois</u>

My first encounter with the spirit world was when I was aged 11.

I was in bed trying to go to sleep when across from me I saw a figure of a man with a burgundy rose. I didn't know what this was, but I didn't feel scared, just curious as to what it might be. I was 19 when I had my next encounter, and I began to see more and more of the spirit world.

Throughout this chapter, I will give you an insight into some of my encounters with the spirit world and why I believe they are real.

Although, my first experience of the other world happened when I was 11. My encounters really started when I went to see an aura cleanser.

Later that night, after I'd had my aura cleansed, I woke up and looked out of the window. I thought to myself that it must be about 3 O'clock in the morning. Whilst I was lying there, I heard a slight Shuffling sound on the carpet. I immediately looked down the bed to see if the sound could've been my dog, but as I looked down, saw my dog lying there fast asleep. Thinking nothing of it, I closed my eyes, ready to go back to sleep, and that's when I heard the sound again, only this time it was louder. My heart started to race because I knew it had to be something or someone else in the room. I closed my eyes tight and tried to pretend this wasn't happening to me. As I lay there, heart racing, I felt a heaviness on my feet as though someone was pressing down on them. The heaviness continued up my body until it reached my shoulders.

Frightened, I kept my eyes closed, wishing and praying it would go away.

As the pressure reached my shoulders, I felt a sudden hard push which caused me to sink into my mattress as if someone was holding me down. With arms flailing around and legs kicking out, I fought to get this pressure off me. After about a minute, the pressure had gone, and my body was released. Out of breath, I got out of bed and checked the room. Nobody was there, and my dog was fast asleep.

To this day, I still don't know what that was or even know why it happened to me, but it's been since then that I have seen many different things, including spirits, witches and even fairies.

This next encounter happened when I was still living at my parents' house. I'd just moved into my new room downstairs, which was once the garage. It was such a lovely room, very peaceful with no living energy, only mine. As my room was downstairs, I would've taken my things upstairs for a shower. As I was walking upstairs, talking to my brother at the time, I saw an elderly man walk from the hallway into the kitchen. This man was about 80, and approximately 6ft 3in, with white hair, receding to the sides, and he wore a checked brown shirt with a green woollen tank top.

In shock, I ran back down the stairs and into the kitchen. No one was there. I called my brother and told him what had happened. He then told me about the man who used to live there and what he was like.

I believe I saw the ghost of the man who used to live in my parents' house and from the way he walked from the kitchen to the hall I think he still lives there, not knowing he is dead.

Since seeing the old man, I have seen many different things and heard noises which I can't explain, but my next encounter was my scariest yet.

I was living in a flat with my boyfriend. My first little home, and I loved it. It was very quiet at night; the only sound you could hear was the sound of hooting owls.

Whilst I was lying in bed one night, trying to go to sleep, I saw two black, huge eyes looking down at me from the top right-hand corner of my room. Trying to make sense of this creature, I stared back. It was covered in what seemed like tar, which was dripping from its head down onto its body. Stuck inside the tar, there seemed to be leaves and twigs sticking out, sinking with the tar as it fell down its body. Still staring at me, I noticed a pair of hands which were folded across its body. It had long fingers and long pointy nails. The energy that this creature gave off was evil and had come with negative intentions.

As I lay there with black eyes staring straight at me, I tried as much as I could to get rid of it. I said the Lord's Prayer, surrounded myself with white light and in my mind told it to go, but it didn't. I slept with the light on that night but was still aware of its presence. The next night the creature was no longer there, and I was so thankful that it had gone.

Just as I was about to drift off to sleep, I saw another dark figure at the door. I was so frightened that I closed my eyes and prayed again for it to go away. Heart pounding, I opened my eyes and there, standing by my bed, in front of my eyes was this dark figure. My heart was in my mouth. I didn't know what to do so I turned to my boyfriend and screamed for him to turn on the light. Not knowing what was going on, he raced out of bed and turned on the light. I looked back, and it was gone.

It was then that I realised that this creature wasn't going to go away by prayers only. The next day I spoke to my Aunt Louise, who advised me how to spiritually cleanse my flat. To remove this negative energy. Whilst describing the creature, she pointed out that it might have been a witch, and instead of tar, it was mud. This made sense as where I was living was known for its spiritual culture and practice of magic and also because I didn't live far from a bog. Following my aunt's guidance, I opened my windows and burnt sage in each room of the flat. Since then, I never saw the witch again.

My next interesting encounter happened whilst I was on holiday in Portugal. I was in bed asleep and suddenly woke. I looked toward my boyfriend and saw a dark figure standing beside the bed. I immediately woke my boyfriend up, and he turned on the light. Once the light came on, the figure went. I didn't tell my boyfriend what I'd seen as I didn't want to worry him but asked him to keep the light on and went back to sleep.

Whilst I was sleeping, my boyfriend turned off the light and went back to sleep. An hour or so later, he suddenly woke me up and asked me if I was okay. He looked worried, so I asked him what was wrong. He said nothing and turned the light back on.

When we got up the next morning, I asked him what had happened last night. This was when he told me that he woke up and saw a dark figure lying on top of me, and this is when he pushed me to get the dark figure off me. I then told him what I had seen, and we were both shocked as I had seen the same figure standing by the side of his bed. We were both freaked out but glad that this was our last night there and we would be returning home.

A couple of months after our experience in Portugal, we both had another strange experience happen to us at home.

We had just got into bed, ready to go to sleep, when I saw a small, dark figure sitting on top of my chest of drawers by the window. I first thought the small figure was my cat and thought nothing of it until I looked down and saw my cat fast asleep on my bed.

Upon seeing my cat, I shook my boyfriend to wake up and asked him to look over by the window to see if he could see what I could see. He said, 'It's only the cat', and it was then I realised that he could also see this figure. I told him it wasn't our cat as she was sleeping on the bed. He sat up, looked at our cat and looked back at the figure and said, 'what the hell is that'. I said I didn't know, but it looked like a small child sitting with its legs hanging down the set of draws. After my boyfriend saw the figure sitting on the chest of drawers, he got up and turned on the light. Upon doing this, the figure went.

After turning on the lights, he got back into bed. This was when we heard knocking and banging noises all over our flat. This went on or at least 20 minutes. For me, I think the figure was a small child, and the knocking noise was a sign of its mischievous behaviour.

In the morning, I checked on the internet to see what was built before and around the flat, to see if this would explain what we had seen. This is when I found out that next to our flat was a famous home for children, which closed many years before. I had never noticed it before, but upon reading about the home, I knew this child had come from there. We never saw the child again but agreed that what we both saw and heard was real.

My next meeting with something from the spirit world came when we were living in our new home.

Since moving into our new home, I haven't seen many spirits as I think and feel the more positive energy in and around our house. The spirits I have seen don't seem to come with any malice but are drawn to me by my inner light. This is what I think these next two spirits were doing.

I had just gotten into bed when I heard something which sounded like a finger running along the lampshade next to my bed. I looked at the lamp and wondered what it might be. I even thought it could be my cat but knew it couldn't possibly be.

As I was thinking about what the noise might be, I noticed a young girl standing about a foot from my bed. I would say she was about 8 years old; she had long, dark hair and was wearing a white pinafore dress. When I looked at her face, I noticed that she didn't have any

eyes, just black holes and from them, there were back streak
coming from them, which ran down her face. Although that may
seem scary, I didn't feel she had come with any negative energy bu
wasn't sure why she was there.

Whilst wondering why this little girl was standing in front of me,
noticed another small girl standing beside her. She was about !
years old, with light brown hair and was wearing a brown smock
dress. The girl was moving from behind the older girl and then back
again as though she was shy. She did this with a plain expression or
her face. I wondered what they wanted and why they had come to
me. I felt that they were spirits from the late 1800s and had maybe
lived on a farm. Maybe they had died in an accident from the olde
girl's eyes or were just lost in the spirit world. They stayed there the
whole night, and every time I woke; there, they were staring at me
Once morning broke, the girls were gone. I never saw them again
but I hope they found their way to the light and are now happy
together.

From my experiences, I have witnessed many different spirits.
know that there are good and bad spirits, just as there are good and
bad people in the world. However, I cannot explain why my spiri
encounters choose to visit me but what I do know is that I am very
lucky to see all of the things I have seen and believe that there must
be another world or energy level on our earth which explains my
experiences.

The fundamentals

Over the past couple of years, I've been so blessed to have seen many earth beings such as fairies, pixies and other fundamentals, and I can truly say they're such amazing creatures. The experience I am going to write about came to me at night just as I turned off the light to go to sleep. It was then that I saw the realm of the fairies.

The other realm is shown to be a mystical and enchanted place, with small, white orbs floating in the dark green mist that flowed through my room. Within the dark green mist, I saw small purple and white specks of light, which danced past my eyes. It was only when I looked closely at these little, bright specks that I noticed that they had small, pointy faces, ears and noses. Their little faces were cheeky and smiley but flew with such graciousness around the room. They had long, wispy wings, which were twice as big as they were and reflected the light they carried.

Amongst the gracious dancing of the beings, I saw a bigger and stranger-looking creature. This googly-eyed creature was the size of a small child and stood at an opening of a small, brown, wooden door. The creature stood to watch at the door, looking down his long, pointy nose at the flying beings. Whilst the creature was observing the small beings, he had a look of concern on his face. He looked intensely over the door and back without his dark green and brown hat moving from his head.

The gaze of the concerned-looking creature was focusing on a group of fairies climbing on the light shade within my room. As I looked up, I saw some mischievous fairies using their delicate arms to hang upside down off the light shade whilst the others danced merrily around it. Although their brazen yet playful actions had been seen by the stocky creature, they appeared blissfully unaware and carried on enjoying themselves regardless.

As I looked around my room, which had now turned into a mystical haven, I noticed more and more playful fairies getting into mischief. A few were climbing up the curtains, and others were dancing happily on the headboard, but the ones I noticed, in particular, were those that flew so quickly up to my face and then out again. As they flew in and out, they laughed in hysterics as if they knew that they were teasing me. As they got so close, I reached out my hand to touch them, but as I did, they flew away.

This was such a unique and incredible experience, and I feel so special that they showed me their world. These brightly coloured fairies come with such joy and happiness; it's so hard not to like them, and they are a pleasure to watch.

When I first moved to my new house, I woke up to find a tall, broad and very large Viking standing to the left of my bed. The first thing I noticed was his long skirt-type trousers, brown and very worn but covering his enormous legs, and wearing a pair of leathery brown muddy boots.

His hands hung low, and his moustache stuck out like hay. Whilst standing there quietly and with no expression, I noticed one of his large hands was gripping a weapon which had 2 metal sharp sides although the handle wasn't long, just big enough for his large hand.

As I looked further up at this enormous man, I noticed that he was wearing a metal helmet which had a pair of magnificent long cured horns attached to the sides. Although the Viking looked intimidating, I knew he hadn't come with any negativity but with a sense of security for me. Like a guard watching over his village.

5 and a half years later, whilst I was teaching, a local historian came to our school to talk about the village's history. What I then heard was amazing. Where my house is situated was once a Viking village dating back to the Anglo Saxons. Also, half a mile from my house, there was a Viking battle where a Viking burial ground was found full of armour.

After hearing about my village's local history, I honestly believe that the Viking had visited me to let me know that this was once his land and was standing there protecting what he may still think was his.

Chapter 14

Marcella

I came to Birmingham from Dublin in the fifties, one of a large family. My Dad and eldest brother came over before to find us a home, and they bought a house in Birmingham with a sitting tenant.

Mom and Dad had some very tough times as Dad had an accident in Ireland and was off work for some years. I was lucky; being the youngest, I didn't see the tough times the rest of the family experienced. I have very happy memories of my childhood with my siblings, laughing and arguing through the years. Mom had a very gently energy but stood no messing but was always very fair. As a young child, I remember Mom going to see a clairvoyant when I was very young with one of my sisters-in-law, and I think that's where my interest began. I was teased at school because I was Irish and remember being unable to go to the Girl guides from Brownies because I was Irish Catholic. How things have changed, so much for the better now.

I spent many hours listening to the stories about the 'little people from my parents and various relatives. I have always loved Buddha's and purchased my first one from a garden centre over 40 years ago, still have it today. It is made of stone.

About 18 years ago, my niece, Daisy, asked me to go with her to see a lady, Lisa, who read the tea leaves. I had recently changed my purse that day and had not transferred all the bits we carry in them to the new purse, and I had mislaid my old purse. I got in Daisy's car twice but had to go back into the house to find my old purse for some reason which I didn't understand. I found the purse and hrew it in my bag as well as the new purse, and off we went. My tea leaf reading was extremely accurate. A bit later, when we were just chatting, I got the most beautiful smell of flowers and commented on it to Lisa and Daisy, but neither of them could smell this heavenly scent. Lisa said it was my Mom (who had passed), and she was worried about Daisy, who was travelling to Australia on her own. Mom wanted me to give Daisy a medal belonging to her, which I had. This was a little gold disc that one of my siblings had bought for Mom when she had Alzheimer's; it had her name and telephone number on it in case she got lost or confused. Mom wanted me to give this to Daisy for protection whilst she was travelling. The medal was in my old purse, which I couldn't leave home without this night. It was the angels working their magic once again. Daisy still wears this medal today and is extremely spiritual, and has a beautiful cabin in her garden where she gives wonderful therapies.

When we lost our parents, it was a massive loss to us all as we were blessed to have this lovely Mom and Dad who were always there for every one of us. We never had loads of material things, but we had loads of love. I remember the overcoats on the beds, but we always had lots of love, and we were blessed with a great sense of humour.

We often had miraculous medals (a small medal, usually silver with an imprint of Our Lady, we had them as children either pinned to our coats or round our necks on a piece of cotton, most catholic children had them). One day I was sitting in my garden thinking about Mom, and I found one on my lawn. I've no doubt Mom sent this for me; she absolutely loved her garden and her family.

After one of my brothers, whose wife passed away, he was in the shower when he heard music playing his favourite song and traced it to a radio playing in their spare room. He was quite unnerved by this as the radio had not been used for some time and had been stored away. Also, he didn't really believe in things like this or things that "**GO BUMP IN THE NIGHT**". Many years later, he told me he felt his wife around him, and she was trying to tell him something. He felt it was to do with the lottery and took himself off to buy a ticket and nearly collapsed on the way back as he was unwell. He won £3.50 on his ticket, and we had a good laugh about this. However, a couple of weeks later, he had a massive bleed on the brain and passed away. I believe she was around to help him with his passing.

I had my first reading many years ago when a colleague took me to see a medium (JW), and I was immediately hooked, fascinated and found it so interesting. It was several years after this that I met my earth angel, Louise, and she has supported, encouraged and given me so much knowledge during the many times I have sat in a circle with her. The exercises are always so interesting, and we had lots of enjoyment and laughter in our many group sessions. I have grown so much and never realised how close our angels always are. continually ask for guidance, support and protection from the angels, and they have never let me down.

Some 20/30 years ago, Louise invited me to a colour therapy day in Leicestershire, and it was fascinating, and I still believe in this now It is not always appropriate to go to work in bright colours or whatever colour we may need; however, I wear colour underneath my clothing, i.e. socks, camisoles and underwear (got purple knickers on today). When I was young, I remember Mom saying, "always make sure you have clean underwear on in case you have an accident" God forbid I ever have one as the medical staff would need sunglasses' also, there was a beautiful crystal shop at the colour therapy course which began my ever-growing love of crystals. One of my grandchildren often asked to look at my crystal collection, and when they were 2-3 years old, I would often find them playing with my crystals; and I believe this is the next generation of crystal keepers. My granddaughters are very much into their crystals.

I have completed Reiki 1, 2 and my Masters with Louise, and it has given me so much, which I have been able to share with others. I have a cabin in my garden where I have given family and friends therapies. It is under 2 massive oak trees with wonderful energies. I also completed an Indian Head Massage and foot/leg massage. I am now looking to do something else and await direction from above as I'm not sure at the moment, but this is probably due to a traumatic time which started in October 2018, losing a true soul mate. When I sat in a circle with Louise, I have received messages for others in the circle but often didn't want to share this information as they often seemed really absurd. However, Louise always encouraged us to say what we had seen or heard, and it always made sense to someone in the circle. I believe this all comes from my Mom, who was a truly beautiful soul.

I have been blessed with truly genuine, loyal friends but recently lost a very special soul mate to a cruel, brutal disease which she fought so bravely for 14 months, never complaining and always thinking and asking about others to the end even when she couldn't verbally communicate she wrote it down. On the day of her funeral, several things happened, and I do believe it was her playing games. Firstly, the iron wouldn't work for me, but my husband had used it 20 minutes before. The kettle wouldn't work, and I moved it to 3 different sockets, then I returned it to its original socket, and it worked, strange. My hairdryer stopped, and I had to dig out my travel dryer, the next day, my dryer worked fine. Some weeks after her funeral, which was over a month after she passed, I went to see a medium who told me some amazing things and spoke about my friend and said it wasn't her messing with the iron on her funeral day as she never did ironing when she was here which is very true. **"IS THERE ANYBODY THERE?"** I think so.

I met up with an old school friend recently who had worked with Louise many years ago. One day Louise told her to tell her daughter to watch her grandson by the front door, which opened onto a busy road. Several days later, my friend's daughter was coming down her stairs, and her son was opening the front door. She asked him where he was going, and he said to see his Nan, which was across a busy road. She changed the door mechanisms immediately.

Chapter 15

Martin

My name is Martin, and I now work as a trance medium and healer. I got to know Louise through my sister as they worked in the Bookmakers together many years ago. Through a reading my sister had from Louise, she mentioned me and asked if I was going to emigrate; at the time, I had spoken about it but never thought it would be any more than a thought. However, I did emigrate some 30 years later.

On holiday back to England, I met Louise for the first time, and she invited me to sit in a spiritual circle; Louise saw a guide behind me and felt he wanted to speak. This guide was Chou. I chatted to Louise, advising her I was a trance medium; she asked if I would come and do a trance circle for the spiritual group, which I did, and I had great feedback from the group. We have been friends for many years, and Louise asked me if I would do a chapter for her book.

This is the story of some of my spiritual experiences on my journey. I have 2 sisters, and their spiritual journeys have been very different to mine. When I was 24, I decided to leave my birth country and immigrate to another country where I still live today and love the life I have in this country.

My Dad passed away when I was 29, and I felt and saw his presence which was my first spiritual experience. Several years later, I met up with a friend, Alice, who gave me a book and advised me to read it. When reading this book, it felt like a jet of water hit the centre of my head, which I later learned was my crown chakra.

During another meditation, I was aware of something being placed on my crown chakra by spirit. From then I started to hear my name being called when no one was there; this started happening almost weekly at the meditation group. This was such a beautiful confirmation from spirit. I have had many amazing experiences on my spiritual journey.

The day I first met my guide was such a profound experience. I felt I was covered in energy from the spirit, which was unknown to me at this time, and I began to speak in the voice of my guides. He is now my main guide, and his name is Chou. The energy was strong and rich and completely covered my body. Chou spoke through me to the other people in the circle many times after that, humbly and with grace explaining life and the importance of meditation.

My journey continued with other guides, and they started to make themselves known to me. Chou has been a constant guide over the years, always there. He is wise and can talk on any topic in great detail that is sometimes beyond simple understanding. However, he does it with simplicity which makes this easy to understand. Over time when Chou visits, everyone hears birds tweeting and then we are aware of his presence in the room.

As my journey continued, other guides made themselves known to me, and they talked, sang and interacted with anyone willing to listen. Charlie is a different character; I know him as he was called Charlie on the river when he was on the earth plain. He died just before the Titanic sunk, and he lived somewhere in London. He always says he liked the simple things in life, sitting down with a glass of rum, watching the sunset and singing his heart out. When he comes to me through trance, he often sings to the people in the congregation, changing the words somewhat, but it always has a meaning. At times he wakes me up at 5am with a song. Friends have told me that Charlie came to them last night singing to them.

Another guide, Ignatius, came through to speak to a closed group one evening and told them he had written a book which they later researched, and all confirmed the information about the book was accurate. He made his presence known one day as he was curious about our progress but has never left.

All of these have been amazing experiences, which deserve to be spoken about in rich detail.

My spiritual journey has had its highs and lows, some of my friends have changed, and my partner has been totally supportive and understanding. I have gained riches, too many to state and have seen things that some people may never understand or believe. You will gain true friends and will be rich in heart. Don't worry about the destination. Just walk the path and enjoy the beauty.

FROM TINY ACORNS, MIGHTY OAK TREES GROW.

An analogy from my guides:-

As you begin your spiritual journey, you do not need to be shown the whole path straight away. It is just like small stepping stones. The guides have explained it to me like this:-

Imagine you live in a remote jungle village, living a simple life with no electricity or Western conveniences.

Then one night, you need to take a journey from your village; there is no electricity to light your way, but once you get used to the dark, the stars will light your way. It is the same with your spiritual journey as you do not need to know every step you will take, just that you leave and arrive safely. The spiritual path will always guide you.

Chapter 16

Lizzie

Things that have happened to me have been stranger than fiction because this is how my life has been since I was little; things that have happened to me have been stranger than fiction which is why I decided to call this chapter. I remember at the age of about 4 years old, playing in my bedroom, and I would sit on the floor, and I would be completely surrounded by what I can only say were clouds; I was sitting in a cloud, and that happened lots and lots and lots of times. Clouds, why would I be sitting in these fluffy white clouds? At about the same time, I was also experiencing nightly excursions where I would leave my bed and float, and I would float all around the house and down the stairs and into the living rooms. Where eventually, after some time, my parents would find me and take me back to bed, and the same thing would happen regularly during my floating excursions.

I had a very disturbed childhood; when I was 8, my Mother left and took me abroad, where we lived for quite a long time, which was not a pleasant experience. We came back to England when I was about 10½ years old and went to senior school at 11 years and started to do a lot of work with the Art teacher. I did a tremendous amount of work for a period of time for the bye centenary of a school that I was going to, and I spent about half a year drawing and painting huge pictures of Edwardian transport and costumes and filled nearly 2 files of these drawings, they were life-size actually, but I enjoyed every minute of it, plus I was excused from all lessons to do this work which suited me fine.

My Mother decided to leave when I was about 12, and I was left at home with my Father, and my Mother disappeared. At the age of nearly 16, she came back, by which time I had quite a good job and was happy in my own company and just shortly after her coming back to this country I met someone who I later married at the age of 17 and had my first child. My Mother, in the meantime, disappeared again, and I was then living with my husband and my first child. Not long after this, I discovered I was pregnant, and we bought a house.

I had 1 or 2 strange dreams. In the first dream I had, my husband said I must have been a witch. We lived next to a nice couple who we became quite friendly with. One night I dreamt that I followed them to a funeral, and after the funeral, I was floating like I used to float when I was a child. I was floating over what appeared to be a banquet with loads of people all eating what looked to be a very expensive meal sitting around a long table. Suddenly, one man who was sitting at the table got up and staggered backwards, and the next thing I was floating above my next-door neighbours who were following a funeral. The next morning I told my husband about this floating dream, this odd occurrence and thought no more about it until a couple of days later, we were pulling on to our drive as they were pulling on to their drive. I called out hello and asked why they were not at work today. They said they had just been to his Dad's funeral. He had died at a big party. So what I had dreamt was right, and my husband then said I was a witch. I am unable to remember the numerous occasions this happened, but it happened regularly. I just got on with living my life with 2 children, and then the third one came along, and I was very busy with the children. However, life was not very good with this husband, who was quite violent at times, and it got worse over time, but looking back, I think he was suffering from depression. He was like this for a few years and had been for some time; as a result of this, I thought it was best for us to split up. I managed to get accommodation for myself and 3 children, and he went back to live with his Mother. Life was very busy and hard at times financially and very alone with the children.

I started to experience a recurring dream where I was going on a journey following a car, and this journey was quite real; virtually, I could describe the route, and I would have recognised the area if I had gone there. I always arrived at a building, and there was a door and windows, and the lights were on. I knew there were people inside, but I could never go through the door. I had a friend at the time who I told about my dream in great detail, and it happened quite a lot over time. However, as time went by, I started to get curious about all the things that had happened in my life. Eventually, I started to attend a Spiritual Church where I would sit in a circle with other people. I discovered I had quite a lot of psychic ability whilst sitting in Circle. I became even more curious, and eventually, whilst being in this church, I was asked to attend another place.

One particular night I was shown the way to go by someone who was taking me, and I had to follow them, and I soon realised that this was the dream I had previously had that was so familiar, and I knew what was coming at the end of it as I was driving behind this car. Eventually, we came to our destination, and there was the building from my dream with the lights on and the door in the middle, which was shut; however, this time, I went through the door, and it was another spiritualist church. I was amazed at how clear the dream was, and it brought me to this place. It definitely was meant to be.

The people at this church were very nice, and I got on really well with them. After many months of attending this church, the lady who actually ran this circle said to me one night, "you are going to work on a platform, but it won't be doing clairvoyance as you will be drawing people that have passed over. I was a bit amazed at this but accepted what she said and carried on as normal. However, in the meantime, I had become very friendly with a lady who was a therapist, and when I went into the room for treatment, I knew her as she was so familiar. As a result of my going for this treatment, we became lifelong friends, and she felt that she knew me. As a result of knowing her, I ended up working with her at the clinic that she ran, and during the time I worked with her helping her in her therapy clinic, we went to a lecture on near-death experiences in a crypt. At the end of the lecture, a lady came in who was coming in to give us a lecture on herbal remedies, which I thought would be interesting. She started to talk about these remedies, and I was absolutely amazed at what she was saying and felt this was something I had to do. No sooner had I got back to my ordinary life than I made it my business to find out everything I could about these herbal remedies. I went into a programme of education and learned everything there was to know about them and how to use them. I then became a practitioner after attending a lot of education and took an exam to become a practitioner, and I used this very successfully in my friend's clinic. In the meantime, I am still living my domestic life. I then met my present husband, and we were living together and jogging along quite happily. My youngest child was then about 8, and I was trying to get him to bed one night, but he didn't want to go saying I'll go to bed if you draw me a tiger which I felt was a strange request. However, if it will get him into bed, I'll try. He sat on the arm of my chair whilst I was trying to draw this tiger. While I was trying to do this tiger, I had this feeling come over me that I was going to draw something else, and it happened quite spontaneously, and out of the blue, I started to draw what appeared to be a young man whose face seemed to get bigger and bigger, and I knew that this face was someone that my husband knew as I recognised this drawing, but the tiger never got finished. The room was very quiet; I turned to my husband and asked him if he knew this person. He said yes, it was a friend of his who died when he was about 17 years old. They had been on holiday, and he died as a result of an illness in hospital. He recognised him immediately. This was the beginning; not only was I doing herbal remedies and seeing people who came to me with various emotional and physical difficulties. The success rate of these remedies was phenomenal, but not only this, but I was also drawn to working in this church, and it went on from there.

Eventually, I was introduced to Louise, and from the moment I met her, I knew I would work with her with these drawings and her clairvoyance. I told her about what I was doing, and it just went from there; we did several churches, and my drawings were always recognised. How this happened, I do not know, as it wasn't something I had set out to do, which is why I called this chapter Stranger than Fiction. It just happened quite; naturally, I have often wondered why. Once, an elderly lady came to me and had a picture of her deceased husband when he was a young man, and she said you will never know what this has done for me, but it had helped her. So is this the reason for doing these drawings, as it helped her at that particular point in their life?

There have been lots of episodes where things have just spontaneously happened, and I have been amazed. On one occasion, my second eldest son, who was married and his wife was diagnosed with cancer and had extensive chemotherapy; she was very ill and was lucky to survive. I took her to all her chemotherapy sessions and appointments with the specialist, and I was there the day they told her she would never have children as she would be sterile due to the chemotherapy. This was extremely sad for them and also for me, but I was a bit philosophical as I had my children but felt it was a great pity this wasn't going to happen for them. At this particular time, we had a caravan and used to go regularly for weekends or any spare moments. On one occasion, we were driving there on a lovely sunny day. I was dropping off to sleep when I had a vision of this daughter-in-law sitting with a little girl about 2 years old on her lap, her hair just reaching her shoulders. Sitting next to her was my only daughter. She also had a child who was a year younger than this little girl. My daughter had been having IVF unsuccessfully for a number of years; however, I knew this child was a boy born when this little girl was 2. I must have been desperate for grandchildren, and I told my husband about it and said it must have been wishful thinking on my part as I knew she couldn't have children, and I didn't think my daughter would.

One weekend we came back late from a trip, around midnight, and outside the house were my son and this daughter-in-law, and they asked us to come in and sit down; this made me very concerned. They said they had something to tell us and my heart sank as thought cancer may have come back. It was the news to tell me she was pregnant, that a miracle had occurred, and this girl who was sterile due to chemotherapy was having a baby. I couldn't believe it and then I remembered the vision I had, and in time she gave birth to a little girl. At the hospital, the nurses called her a miracle baby and took her around the hospital, showing her to everybody. When this little miracle was 2 years old, my daughter gave birth to her son, just as my vision had shown me. This amazed me as I wasn't asleep, and I saw it just as it later happened, which I think is stranger than fiction; you just couldn't possibly make these things up, especially as this wasn't meant to happen, which really makes you think about life. About people who have been long gone can appear on paper exactly as they were, what causes this to happen, the dreams and all this knowing things are going to happen?.

I was sitting in a circle having meditation one night, and I saw a lovely beach and a man was leaning up a palm tree really relaxed, sitting crossed-legged, and there was a gorilla in front of him. How could I possibly tell the others in the group what I had seen? When it came to my turn to tell the group if I had seen anything, I felt embarrassed to tell the group what I had seen, but I had to. After I finished explaining my vision, the lady sitting opposite me said that it would be my Uncle, who was head keeper at a zoo and the gorilla was his favourite, and they were very close. I was absolutely amazed. Always say what you see in your spiritual visions.

Chapter 17

Crystal Children

In the last few years, families are noticing that a lot of our children are becoming very interested in crystals. In the last 12 months, my granddaughter, Lisa, has started looking to buy crystals and when on holiday, we came upon a lovely crystal shop and decided to go in and purchase some crystals. She wanted some crystals to gain confidence to get a part-time job whilst at college. I advised her she would need the 3 base chakra colours, Red Jasper for a base, Carnelion for the sacral centre and Tigers Eye for solar plexus. I asked her to handle the crystals to see if she felt their energy. When she chose her crystals and handled them, she actually swayed. We purchased them and cleansed them when we got home, and she started holding the crystals and sending her thoughts to gain more confidence to enable her to get a job. She filled in 5 application forms and sent them off to 5 different companies. She was offered employment at all the companies she sent her applications to and chose one in retail. She truly believes the crystals have inspired and boosted her confidence. She has since purchased pink heart-shaped quartz. On the first day of wearing it to college, she sat next to Ollie, and one of her gay friends asked her to ask Ollie if he fancied him. He said no, but I do fancy you and asked her to come on a date, and they have been together since.

My grandson, Joe, came on a visit earlier this year, and we were chatting about Lisa getting her new job with the help of the crystals.

We visited a crystal shop to see how Joe would feel using the crystals. Upon picking some crystals up, he felt woozy and out of balance but also connected to their energies. We purchased several different crystals. He felt a burning sensation in his 3rd eye; it then changed to feeling warm, soothing and relaxing. In the evening, he asked me to give him some healing on some discomfort in his lower back. I asked him to give me the colours he saw during the healing. He immediately got green, and I was sending him green energy. After healing Joe, I gave his brother some healing, and he also told me the colours I was using.   Joe is still using the crystals and has started to pick up energy and colours around people. Also, lately, he has started to see the energy from the elementals, a fairy with very large wings. She tried to communicate with him, but he couldn't fully understand.

There was a surprise in store for Joe at the college he attends. He entered a competition in his class to win £3,000 to put towards a project he is interested in, which is producing films with special effects. He was 'over the moon' to find out he had won the competition. The money will go towards spending time with a large filming company where he will stay with them for 2 weeks in a different country. How amazing is this, the crystals working their magic once again?

In talking to friends and family, I have been told that a lot of their children and grandchildren are becoming very interested in crystal energies. Amazed by their touch and colours.

Chapter 18

COVID

Towards the end of 2019, I could feel a change of energy coming in for the world and kept thinking and saying to people that something awful was going to happen; however, I was unable to pick up what it was.

One day I was in my healing room and saw the name of a country drawn on the wall in smoky writing and wondered what this meant. I soon found out it was Covid which brought the countries on the earth plane to a standstill and life as we know it to an abrupt end. People were dying in their hundreds, and we were so frightened to go out, and the country was locked down for 14 weeks. My family did our shopping and left it on the front garden path; we then had to wash everything before it could be put away. The only thing that helped was the lovely weather in April/May, which enabled us to sit in the garden with no aeroplanes flying over and hardly any cars on the road. It was like another world, and the news was very frightening, with so many people dying day after day.

When the numbers started to drop, it was lovely to be able to get out for walks with the family, take a flask and some cake and just sit in the park, things we just always took for granted.

Also, the spiritual energies have changed as well since the Age of Aquarius, which started in March 2021, opening our hearts to neighbours, friends, and charities in parts of the world that are suffering greatly from starvation and pollution, also the ice sheets melting in the Arctic. People in flat-lying countries are being flooded, homes being under threat of flooding and losing livestock. Working together to save the planet and the human race is the only way forward. **The greed for money and war is not the right energies to go forward with now.**

Thinking about the animal kingdom and the way man shoots and kills for sport is not the right thing anymore. Animals have as much right on this planet earth as a man as they were here before man. The oceans with so much plastic being poured into them make it a dumping ground for mankind, and it will not tolerate being used like this.

The younger generation is now standing up to stop this because it is not the world they want to inherit. It is essential we all get together and think about what we are doing to this paradise we live in and educate our children. Beautiful flowers, trees, beaches and tropical paradises. Our earth feeds everybody and every animal living on this earth every day. We are alive down here because of the bounty of food she produces daily. However, with climate change, fires and floods on the earth, man must look at the error of his ways before it is too late.

Some good things have come out of COVID, i.e. people joining zoom meetings which I have done myself with spiritual circles and meeting with other mediums to carry on with clairvoyance and still getting visions and guidance coming back in so we could give readings and send healing to each other on zoom.

Meeting people from different countries, I would never have me
without zoom.

MAKING FRIENDS AROUND THE WORLD
IS AMAZING.

WATCH THIS SPACE

Does the Human Race realise

"Only when the last fish is
caught
will we realise we cannot eat
money".

ARCHANGEL MICHAEL PRAYER
FOR PROTECTION

LORD MICHAEL BEFORE

LORD MICHAEL BEHIND

LORD MICHAEL TO THE RIGHT

LORD MICHAEL TO THE LEFT

LORD MICHAEL ABOVE

LORD MICHAEL BELOW

LORD MICHAEL LORD MICHAEL

WHEREVER I GO

Say three times

It's a Mantra

Printed in Great Britain
by Amazon

34324016R00086